THE UNRULY NOTION
OF ABUSE OF RIGHTS

Everyone condemns what they perceive as 'abuse of rights', and some would elevate it to a general principle of law. But the notion seldom suffices to be applied as a rule of decision. When adjudicators purport to do so, they expose themselves to charges of unpredictability, if not arbitrariness. After examining the dissimilar origins and justification of the notion in national and international doctrine, and the difficulty of its application in both comparative and international law, this book concludes that except when given context as part of a *lex specialis*, it is too nebulous to serve as a general principle of international law.

JAN PAULSSON is Emeritus Professor at the School of Law of the University of Miami and a former Centennial Professor at the London School of Economics. He has served as President of the London Court of International Arbitration, the International Council for Commercial Arbitration, and the World Bank Administrative Tribunal; and as a Vice-President of the ICC International Court of Arbitration. He is a Member of the Permanent Court of Arbitration in The Hague. He is the author of *The Idea of Arbitration* (2013) and *Denial of Justice in International Law* (2005).

T0381621

THE UNRULY NOTION OF ABUSE OF RIGHTS

JAN PAULSSON
Three Crowns LLP

CAMBRIDGE
UNIVERSITY PRESS

CAMBRIDGE
UNIVERSITY PRESS

University Printing House, Cambridge CB2 8BS, United Kingdom

One Liberty Plaza, 20th Floor, New York, NY 10006, USA

477 Williamstown Road, Port Melbourne, VIC 3207, Australia

314-321, 3rd Floor, Plot 3, Splendor Forum, Jasola District Centre, New Delhi - 110025, India

103 Penang Road, #05-06/07, Visioncrest Commercial, Singapore 238467

Cambridge University Press is part of the University of Cambridge.

It furthers the University's mission by disseminating knowledge in the pursuit of education, learning and research at the highest international levels of excellence.

www.cambridge.org
Information on this title: www.cambridge.org/9781108814836
DOI: 10.1017/9781108887229

First published 2020
First paperback edition 2022

A catalogue record for this publication is available from the British Library

ISBN 978-1-108-84069-9 Hardback
ISBN 978-1-108-81483-6 Paperback

Cambridge University Press has no responsibility for the persistence or accuracy of URLs for external or third-party internet websites referred to in this publication, and does not guarantee that any content on such websites is, or will remain, accurate or appropriate.

For Marike and Samuel – two miracles in a single lifetime . . .

CONTENTS

FOREWORD: THE THESIS AND A CONFESSION

Anyone who has read Jean-Daniel Roulet's *Le caractère artificel de la théorie de l'abus de droit en droit international public* will wonder how the notion of the prohibition of abuse of right as a general principle survived its publication in 1958, five years after the appearance of Bin Cheng's famous *General Principles*. Cheng's book contained a chapter on good faith, which he indeed posited as a general principle. Its subtitle, appearing within parentheses, extended the discussion to what the author referred to modestly as the *theory* of abuse of right. Yet this is perhaps the single most important basis for the common belief that the notion is, in fact, a general principle. Roulet, a Swiss scholar who had pursued his graduate studies under Cheng in London, reached an emphatically negative conclusion: 'By reason of the primitive and often imprecise character of the rules of international law, the theory of abuse of right, itself characterised by considerable elasticitiy and imprecision, loses all utility in the context of international law.'

It is noteworthy that Cheng was invited to write the preface to Roulet's work, and even more important to note that Cheng was laudatory and indeed, in so many words, declined to take a position as to 'the place of the *theory* of abuse of right in international law'. (A more detailed discussion of the two authors' analysis of the subject appears in the part of Chapter 2 entitled 'Reading Bin Cheng Properly'.)

Yet Cheng continues to be cited as an authority for the proposition that abuse of right is a general principle, while *Le caractère artificiel* is largely forgotten. One reason is that Roulet abandoned the path of scholarship for a long and successful career at the World Bank, and did not spend time developing and defending his thesis. Another is simply that he wrote in French. In any event, countless lawyers have continued to invoke the notion of abuse of right in their pleadings. But when judges and arbitrators address the topic, it seems most often to explain why a particular fact pattern does *not* constitute an abuse of right, and so its existence tends to be posited in dicta rather than given effect by a holding.

But far more disturbing is the fact that it is also enlisted as a convenient way to justify an outcome that fails to find a basis in anything that resembles pre-existing criteria which can be considered as rules of decision. Thus the impetus of this book – to insist that the pretense of using a nebulous abstraction as the sole justification for a decision is the path to arbitrariness and disaffection for international law.

It is, of course, easy to agree that conduct amounting to the abuse of a right is wrong. But this does not help us decide anything, given the endless variety of opinions as to what constitutes abusive conduct. Is malice necessary, or is it enough to find disproportionality between the right asserted and the harm caused? Indeed, what is 'harm'? Could it not include the enforcement of ordinary contractual rights that have turned out to be disadvantageous to the respondent? What is one to make of a claim that a right is not being used for its intended purpose, if 'purpose' is inevitably left to the eye of the beholder? As we shall see (in Chapter 3), it takes no great effort to identify more than thirty competing formulations of abuse of right. If we are to know where we stand, it seems that abuse of right must be generated by a *lex specialis*, be it a statute or treaty, which defines abuse of the rights it creates by reference to identified criteria or explicitly accords adjudicatory discretion where it seems contextually indispensable.

Conceivably, in some ideal system, 'abuse of right' could operate as a free-standing rule of decision established by a rigorous and stable *jurisprudence constante*, needing no statute or treaty, but there seems to be no chance that this will occur at the international level. In truth, the judicial hesitations and contradictions within individual national legal systems hardly show much promise there either.

The thesis of this book is that the notion of abuse of right, whatever sympathy one may have for the idealistic impulses of its proponents, cannot be the foundation for a general principle of law or an acceptable rule of decision on the international plane. As an *analytical matter*, the conclusion that there has been an abuse of right is either redundant because the claimed right is in any event rejected by reference to other rules of decision, or else necessarily dealt with according to the personal preferences of the decision-maker. As *a matter of policy*, which is of particularly acute concern in the field of international law, decisions that amount to case-by-case rule-making by adjudicatory bodies may engender hostile reactions and weaken general adherence to the law.

The only place for the notion of abuse of right is therefore when a law-maker determines that a certain type of right may generate temptations that are difficult to foresee and define, therefore justifying an explicit *legislated* grant of adjudicatory discretion to decide based on either broad considerations or specific criteria. But when such discretion is granted, the general expression *abuse of right* adds nothing; anyone assigned authority to assess the contested exercise of a right on a discretionary basis will not need to be told to reject abuse.

Yet I must confess to having practiced and taught law for many years without questioning the status of abuse of right as a general principle of law. Nor, I must further admit and will now explain, was it my first-discovered blind spot.

More than two decades had passed since the end of my formal law studies (in the United States and France) when I began grappling with the notion of *denial of justice* as a member of the arbitral tribunal in a case usually referred to as *Azinian* v. *Mexico*.[1] It was not the only issue in the case; the legal authorities put before the tribunal were not exhaustive; the submissions by the parties exposed many difficulties. I was sufficiently familiar with the concept to know that non-lawyers, who frequently and with great fervour employ the term *denial of justice* when they comment on public affairs, generally misuse it as a synonym for *injustice* – to be freely enlisted as a criticism of any court decisions with which they strongly disagree. But when I was confronted with this concrete case, I came to see complexities that had never occurred to me before, which continued to puzzle me even after we had unanimously resolved the matter before us.

This experience motivated me to write a book called *Denial of Justice in International Law*. The present volume has a similar genesis.

Abuse of right turns out to be a more elusive subject. Indeed, it could be dismissed – and has been dismissed – as useless nonsense; only lawyers, it might be said, could find it a struggle to understand the idea that if you go beyond what you are allowed to do, you are not allowed to do it. To understand whether a right has evaporated by the transgression of its boundaries, it is surely better to be able to invoke autonomous rules that define the abusive conduct one wishes to discourage – like those that pertain to neighbourhood nuisance. Why would we need to say that people who play deafening music through the night in a residential area are 'abusing their rights' as homeowners?

---

[1] *Robert Azinian et al.* v. *The United Mexican States*, ICSID Case No. ARB(AF)/97/2, award, 1 November 1999, 5 *ICSID Reports* 269.

Here, too, my interest in the subject was piqued by a case that I was involved with as an arbitrator, often referred to as *Himpurna v. Indonesia.*[2] One of my colleagues on that tribunal joined me in concluding that the damages sought were excessive (1) insomuch as they related exclusively to lost profits to be gained under an infrastructural investment project yet to be commenced, given moreover the facts that (2) the arbitrators agreed unanimously to grant significant lost profits with respect to the investments actually made by the claimants and that (3) a worldwide economic crisis had created a situation in which further performance would have caused immense and certain losses to the respondent, as well as ever-greater hardship to the people of Indonesia. We wrote that 'abuse of right' was a general principle of law (Indonesian law was applicable, and my colleague in the majority was a retired judge of the Supreme Court of Indonesia) and that to seek the full enforcement of contractual rights under these circumstances would be abusive. The dissenter succinctly expressed his failure to understand how reliance on a perfectly lawful contract could be abusive. (Some further observations about *Himpurna* may be found in Chapter 4.)

In the two following decades, I have suffered no qualms about the outcome in that case. A significant feature of the contracts in question was a provision to the effect that 'the Tribunal need not be bound by strict rules of law' and the arbitrators were authorised to use their discretion as to the 'correct and just enforcement of this agreement'. Yet I am now of a different mind as to the soundness of our unnecessary invocation of the notion of abuse of right. I may perhaps say in mitigation that arbitrators operate under the constraints of the record before them and of the need (in most cases) for the agreement of at least two members of the tribunal. At any rate, I developed an abiding curiosity about the concept of abuse of right and began taking notes for what has become this volume. I have come to recant my assumption in *Himpurna* that the notion can claim a place as a general principle of law – as opposed to a pithy abstraction enlisted to justify an outcome.

This book makes no pretence of being a systematic exposition of comparative law (a field in which I am but a modest amateur). It is concerned with broader concepts. Examples from national legal systems are used as illustrations, without worrying whether they are consonant

---

[2] *Himpurna California Energy Ltd.* v. *Republic of Indonesia*, interim award, 26 September 1999; final award, 16 October 1999; extracts in 25 *ICCA Yearbook Commercial Arbitration* (2000), 109, 186.

with current jurisprudence or legislation. Yet these illustrations are not fictional, and that is important because 'general principles of law', in order to be recognised as a source of international law, must be derived from *common* norms established by national legal systems. The notion of abuse of right fails in this respect as a result of its heterogeneity and indeterminateness – powerful evidence that it does not merit recognition as an autonomous category of breach of international law.

'To speak of an abuse of a right without attempting to determine its nature is simply to indulge in a rhetorical flourish which finds its only echo in an empty phrase. Some definite criterion is required...'

H. C. Gutteridge, 'Abuse of Rights', 5 *Cambridge Law Journal* (1933), 22.

1

Matters of Nomenclature

'Concepts', 'Principles', and 'Rules'

In his familiar study *General Principles*,[1] Cheng did not refer to abuse of right as a 'principle' but a theory. Indeed, the words 'abuse of right' seek to convey nothing more than a concept. They cannot literally define a principle any more than the two words 'negligence' or 'murder' could do so. To state a principle, one would have to add something like '... is wrong' or, depending on the context, '... unlawful'. (That this may be obvious, given the pejorative connotations inherent in the word 'abuse', is another matter.)

As the simple designation of a topic for discussion, abuse of right may be referred to indifferently as a *notion, concept, idea,* or *theory.* The expression, it seems fair to say, assumes that rights may in fact be abused, although that is not much of an insight; of course rights may be abused.

A *principle* expresses a judgment. The Ten Commandments provide familiar illustrations – for example, *thou shall not* take the name of the Lord thy God in vain; *thou shall* honour thy father and mother. A principle may be expressed more gently: 'honesty is the best policy'. The principle associated with the expression *abuse of rights* is that it should be forbidden.

The question then becomes whether a concept endowed with a value judgment, and thus entitled to be referred to as a principle, should become a rule of law.[2] Some ancient principles, like *an eye for an eye,*

---

[1] B. Cheng, *General Principles of Law as Applied by International Courts and Tribunals* (Cambridge University Press, 1953; paperback, 2006); see the subtitle used by Cheng for chapter 4.

[2] Consider the bold-faced words of a United States Supreme Court judgment rendered in early 2019: 'The phrase "immunity enjoyed by foreign governments" is not a term of art

are now rejected. Others, however morally solid, are nevertheless unsuitable as rules of law. We teach our children not to lie, but we do not have a law that forbids lying because it would be too indeterminate, creating endless disputation unworthy of the attention of public institutions. Of course, there are innumerable laws that punish dishonesty in specific circumstances. They reflect disapproval and indeed sanctions of various types of prevarication, but do not make lying punishable in general.

So, rights can be abused, and the abuse of rights is to be condemned. There are laws that reflect intolerance of the abuse of rights in particular circumstances. Of course, such laws are confirmations of the principle that the abuse of rights is not acceptable, but that confirmation is superfluous; we know it already. The significant question is rather whether the existence of such laws proves the existence of a general principle of law *applicable without further specificity as a rule of decision.*

Specific rules, whether established by the law-maker or by long-established judicial pronouncements which the legislature has seen no reason to amend, would not be necessary in a legal system that contented itself with the broad principle of the unlawfulness of abuse of rights because it can rely on a stratum of well-understood specific underlying criteria to provide implicit rules of decision. The thesis of this book is that few, if any, legal systems – and certainly not the international one – can make such a claim and that the notion of abuse of rights is therefore unsuitable as a universal rule of decision because of its irremediable indeterminateness, which leads to open-ended discretion and unpredictability.

This is not to say that a rule of decision may not be broad. The law of civil responsibility for torts seems to function without granular rules as to whether conduct is negligent, or that at some point negligence is aggravated. The finder of fact is trusted to examine the factual circumstances and, being a member of a given society, endowed with shared notions of acceptable conduct, able to assess the reasonableness of behaviour in the circumstances.[3]

But when the legislator has made detailed prescriptions for what is (or is not) wrong-doing or abuse, or anything else that makes it impossible to claim a right, the theory of abuse of right adds nothing (save perhaps confusion). As the great French scholar Marcel Planiol famously

---

with substantive content but rather a **concept** that can be given scope and content only by reference to the **rules** governing foreign sovereign immunity.' See *Jam et al. v. International Finance Corporation*, 586 U.S. – (2019), pp. 9–11.

[3] Still, in systems when the finders of fact are the members of a jury, losing parties may complain on appeal about the trial judge's instructions to the jury, which then, in effect, seem elevated to sub-issues of law.

objected: 'the right ends where the abuse commences'.[4] Numerous scholars in civil law jurisdictions have similarly resisted the theory of abus de droit.[5]

In 1987, thirteen eminent scholars from England and France (mostly from the universities of Paris and Oxford) produced a remarkable treatise of comparative law entitled *Le contrat d'aujourd'hui: comparaisons franco-anglaises*.[6] If *abus de droit* was a general principle of the importance that its adherents seek to give it, one would have expected a conceptual confrontation, or perhaps a rapprochement, of the two systems. To the contrary, the expression appears only fleetingly in the last chapter of the book,[7] devoted to a French *lex specialis* – namely, the special protection against the consequences of abusive termination of automobile dealerships in consideration of the investments typically made by dealers in their businesses, which is the very kind of particularised application of the concept this book endorses.

[4] See Chapter 2, note 22.
[5] A few quotations will suffice. Professor Antonio Gambaro of the University of Milano: 'The doctrine of abuse of rights has a long history but little future', in A. Gambaro, 'Abuse of Rights in the Civil Law Tradition', *European Review of Private Law* (1995), 561; he referred at p. 570 to the doctrine as based on 'a gallery of miseries that are unworthy of such attention by celebrated jurists who should have something better to do'. Professor Antoine Pirovano of the University of Nice, in A. Pirovano, 'La fonction sociale des droits: Réflexions sur le destin des théories de Josserand', 13 *Recueil Dalloz-Sirey Chronique* (1972), 67: 'the "great majority of authors" consider that abuse of right is a "pure application of the general principles of civil liability … simply a tort committed when using a right … we are far from the audacity of Josserand for whom abuse of right was "conduct contrary to the institution, the spirit, and the purpose of law"'. In the sentence following her citation of this very phrase from Josserand, Professor Elspeth Reid of the University of Edinburg: 'The obvious weakness of this wide definition is that it confers a wide discretion on the courts in determining social purpose,' in E. Reid, 'Abuse of Rights in Scots Law', 2 *Edinburg Law Review* (1998), 129, 137; she continued, at p. 141: 'If whenever the individual chooses whether or not to do something, he is exercising a right which is susceptible of abuse, the doctrine of abuse of rights can be extended almost indefinitely. It is being invoked to demand specific performance where there is in fact no underlying obligation.' An extended quotation from the Swiss scholar Jean-Daniel Roulet's comprehensive rejection of the abuse of right as a general principle, J. D. Roulet, *Le caractère artificiel de la théorie de l'abus de droit en droit international public* (Baconnière Neuchatel, 1958), is reproduced in Chapter 2, note 11.
[6] D. Talon and D. Harris (eds.), *Le contrat d'aujourd'hui: comparaisons franco-anglaises* (Librairie générale de droit et de jurisprudence, 1987).
[7] Talon and Harris, *Le contrat d'aujourd'hui*, pp. 331 et seq.; see especially p. 353.

The Particular Unhelpfulness of the Word 'Abuse'

Abuse is always wrong. It is wrong to abuse friendship, or trust, or alcohol. But reaching for an emotive word does not produce a useful legal rule of decision. The law will specify the circumstances in which there has been a fraud, or dissipation of assets intended for underage beneficiaries of a will, or 'driving under the influence' justifying the loss of a driving license or a prison sentence. We all know that 'abuse of process' is not to be tolerated, but the phrase itself leads nowhere until it is given some specificity, as when trial judges identify and reject 'vexatious' or 'oppressive' procedural tactics.

When licensed automobile drivers commit traffic violations, it would not occur to anyone to say that they have *abused their right* as licensed drivers. The rules of the road define the relevant rights, irrespective of licenses. Just so, a building contractor may be entitled to increase his price if the cost of the specified marble increases, but there is no reason to say that he *abuses his right to be paid* if he demands an exaggerated price. The straightforward position is that he had no right to make a claim for anything more than the objective inflation of the price of marble; beyond that point, he had no right that he could abuse. An excessive *demand* may well be said to be abusive, particularly if the circumstances suggest an element of extortion, but the word 'abuse' expresses a value judgment rather than a legal characterisation, and the non-existent right plays no part of the discussion. When the law explicitly identifies particular terms of contract as unenforceable (whether using qualifications such as 'unfair', 'unconscionable', or the like), it is unnecessary and therefore pointless to say that it is an abuse of right to invoke them. (Of course, it then becomes necessary to develop a more specific understanding of *those* qualifications, which happens naturally in the particular context of their application.)

Similarly, we do not need to say that persons living on a residential street *abuse their right* as homeowners if they produce deafening noise throughout the night; they simply do not have the right to create a nuisance.

The notion of abuse of right is obviously problematic. Is the term nonetheless justifiable and does it fill a gap which would become evident if we ceased using it? This is a debatable question, and will be given the fullest attention in the pages that follow. But the answer to the next question – namely, 'What does it matter?' – should be clear. It is this: we should be careful about elevating unnecessary abstractions to the status of fundamental principles, because they contribute to unpredictability and arbitrariness. They also encourage imprecise legislation that leaves citizens and other subjects of the law uncertain of their rights and obligations. The rule of judges is not the rule of law.

Planiol, who as we shall see in Chapter 2 was an unbeliever, regretted the popularity of the word *abus*, which, he wrote, *a fait fortune* ('has struck it rich') in the context of a lively debate among French scholars that began in the 1890s. The most prominent promoter of the theory – Louis Josserand – would himself have preferred the term *détournement de droit*. (This expression is difficult to translate out of context; common uses like *détournement de fonds*, i.e., embezzlement, or *détournement d'avion*, i.e., airplane hijacking, suggest 'misappropriation' or simply 'misuse'.) Marc Desserteaux, a specialist of comparative law (unlike his French colleagues Planiol and Josserand), considered that *abus de droit* could equally be considered as 'the conflict of rights', *conflit de droit*, a rather ingenuous suggestion since it describes the typical reason for the dispute that has arisen, in either national or international contexts.[8] (A property owner's right to build collides with his neighbour's right of access to sunlight; the territorial sea of two states overlap.)

A few decades later, the prominent English comparatist H. C. Gutteridge wrote that for the purposes of his commentary 'we may conveniently adopt the phrase "abuse of rights" because it emphasises the underlying conception that the law should prohibit the exercise of a right for a purpose which shocks the conscience of mankind'.[9] No one can disagree with this formulation as a statement of principle, but of course in and of itself it is no more than a 'rhetorical flourish' (see the epigram that introduces this Chapter). Yet, as we shall see in Chapter 3, there are countless definitions that achieve no more than this and thus give us only what Gutteridge called 'empty phrases'.

At any rate, the expression 'abuse of rights' is no more self-defining than 'negligence' or 'murder'. To kill a human being *may* be murder – but not necessarily. What if a disturbed individual dashes into the middle of a busy highway and is hit by a motorist who was obeying all the rules of the road? Even negligence on the part of the driver would not lead to a finding of murder, given the absence of an intent to crash into the victim. What if the defendant in a murder trial had been a protagonist in

[8] M. Desserteaux, 'Abus de droit ou conflit de droit', *Revue trimestrielle de droit civil* (1906), 337.

[9] H. C. Gutteridge, 'Abuse of Rights', 5 *Cambridge Law Journal* (1933), 22.

a bar-room quarrel who punched a stranger, causing him to fall awk-wardly and break his neck? (Although the *impact* was intended, the *result* was not.) We certainly distinguish between an impulsive altercation and a premeditated deadly attack. None of this is simple; it requires distinc-tions among a group of concepts like 'manslaughter', 'wrongful death', and 'involuntary homicide', not to mention the other refinements of 'degrees' of culpability leading to consequences that are understood only by persons well acquainted with the applicable law.

Nor is 'negligence' self-defining. Although the concept cannot be transformed into mechanically applicable prescriptions, this does not mean that it signifies whatever the particular trier of fact may think of as careless. In jurisdictions where this is decided by a jury, the judge gives instructions as to the standards they should apply, and a mistaken instruction may result in a reversal for misapplication of the law. And if it becomes necessary in a particular national court to assess the tortiousness of conduct in accordance with the law of a foreign jurisdic-tion where the jury system is not used in civil matters, experts will certainly be able to give better answers, notably by reference to patterns observed in prior judgments, than to say that 'negligence is whatever the court finds to be careless'.

With such examples, we must also consider the concept of remedies and sanctions. Here again, the law gives better answers than 'whatever the judge feels is right'. In one case, the judge will be informed by the Criminal Code as to the meaning and consequences of *mens rea*; in the other, he will have to consider things like the distinction between direct and consequential damages – and, in some jurisdictions, the possibility of punitive damages.

Suffice it to say that the words 'abuse of right is unlawful' cannot provide the *ratio* to decide a single case unless there are adequately acknowledged definitions of the conduct that falls under it. The word 'unlawful' is also equally useless unless the consequences are defined. The project to establish a general principle of abuse of right fails in both respects, for reasons that do not permit the expectation that it will ever succeed in the international community as we know it today.

The crux of the problem seems to lie in the single word 'abuse'. It is a part of everyday language, conveying many different meanings. Most of them contain a value judgment that has no legal consequence. *Abusing* someone's generosity is poor manners. *Substance abuse*, such as the excessive consumption of alcohol or prescription medicine, will be rep-rimanded by the doctor. Neither type of behaviour is, in most countries, a matter for the judge. *Child abuse* is a different matter. And judges, when applying laws that *explicitly* call for equitable or discretionary assessments, may use the word 'abusive' to describe unreasonable conduct. There is abuse of process, abuse of office, abuse of discretion – the list goes on. Judges cannot simply wave a wand, recite the words 'abuse of right', and pretend that they have satisfied the obligation to give a legal basis for deciding in favour of a party which has displeased them.

The diffuse senses of the word muddy the waters. They may impede a proper understanding of principles intended to justify or deny legal remedies, because such principles require specific constitutive elements that generate legal security for those who are subject to the law and seek security by acting in accordance with them.

Four Alternative Uses of the Word

If we do not take the trouble to be precise in identifying the features of behaviours we wish to regulate, we experience them, to quote William James's famous phrase, 'all as one great blooming, buzzing confusion'. James was a prominent American intellectual figure of the late nineteenth century in the fields of philosophy and psychology. He reasoned that our minds must be trained by both association and disassociation; the former being necessary for synthesis, the latter for analysis: 'Any number of impressions, from any number of sensory sources, falling simultaneously on a mind which has not yet experienced them separately, will fuse into a single undivided object for that mind. The law is that all things fuse that can fuse, and nothing separates except what must.' And so on to the famous passage: '[T]he baby, assailed by eyes, ears, nose, skin, and entrails at once, feels it all as one great blooming, buzzing confusion.'[10]

'Nothing separates except what must.' James's 'law' continues to be debated by psychologists, but is surely a useful thought to be kept in mind for legal analysis. Just so, four uses of the word *abuse* must be 'separated' (distinguished). Only the fourth should ever be used as part of the expression 'abuse of rights' – and even that one does not generate an autonomous rule of decision.

The first is a way to characterise conduct by reference to inevitably subjective standards such as reasonableness – for example, in connection with an obligation to give reasonable notice or the prohibition of

---

[10] W. James, *Principles of Psychology* (Henry Holt and Company, 1890); see chapter 13 ('Discrimination and Comparison'), p. 483.

unreasonable restraint of trade. If a judge declares that the notice is *abusively* short, or that the territorial scope of a non-compete clause has *abusive* consequences, there is no need to speak of 'abuse of rights', since the legal standard when applied to the facts as found by the decision-maker (judge, arbitrator, or jury) involves the absence of a right to give such short notice, or to rely on such a broad prohibition.

Instead of using the word 'abusive' in this sense, the decision-maker might have said 'excessive', 'unduly burdensome/onerous', 'oppressive', or the like.

Of course, someone wedded to the expression 'abuse of rights' could insist terminologically on viewing the matter as one of abuse of the 'right' envisaged by contractual stipulations. The point is that it is unnecessary, since the right is limited by specific rules of law. To speak of abuse thus has no utility. To the contrary, it is likely to lead to arbitrariness.

The second use is merely a way of characterising simple unlawfulness. 'Child abuse' is not the abuse of a right; it is simply punishable behaviour. 'Abuse of power' is excess of power and therefore does not involve the exercise of a right. For the reason stated in the preceding paragraph, I hardly need to observe the pedantry that would be involved in insisting that we are talking about the abuse of the *right of custody* and of the *prerogatives of office*. Going down this dogmatic route would turn practically everything into an examination of the abuse of some right – exceeding the speed limit or playing loud music after midnight would be the abuse of a driver's license or of the right of homeownership. Indeed, expressions such as 'abuse of financial regulations' generally mean nothing more or less than violation of the law by disregard, circumvention, or fraud. There is no right involved, whether used or abused. (For the last time: speaking of abusing the right to issue corporate securities, an extensively regulated matter, would be the expression of a pointless *idée fixe*.)

This may be the moment to observe that a key to the occasionally peremptory resistance of the common law to the notion of abuse of right may simply be terminological. In English, 'the law' and 'a right' are separate words for different things. In French, *droit* covers both, as does *Recht* in German. If a common lawyer were told about the principle that one should not 'abuse the law', he might quickly say not only 'of course' but be instinctively convinced that the common law agrees: the law should not be misused.

This leads to the third sense, precisely that of *misuse*. From my adolescence, like anyone raised in the Swedish language, I was aware of the expression *rättsmissbruk*, which is in a lexical sense a cognate to the German *Rechtsmissbrauch* – and assumed not only that both are essentially equivalent to abuse of right but, more importantly, that they are applied in a manner supportive of the concept as a general principle. My subsequent readings have lead me to conclude that we should not leap to the conclusion that *misuse* of a legal process is synonymous with the *abuse* of a right. For example, the right to bring a civil suit does not include vexatious or oppressive actions; they are simply not allowed. Moreover, the two words should be distinguished by the element of intentionality, always present in abuse, not necessarily in misuse.

The most cited study of the subject in Sweden is an essay by Professor Jori Munukka of the Stockholm University Law Faculty, which appeared in 2008 under a title that announces 'a legal concept in progress'.[11] (*Rättsmissbruk,* like *Rechtsmissbrauch*, can be rendered as either 'abuse of law' or 'misuse of law'.) It is an interesting and sober piece of scholarship; much credit should be given to the author for his objective account of judicial pronouncements that clearly disappoint his explicit desire that the concept be adopted in Swedish law. For example, the essay's second sentence is instructive; it acknowledges that the expression 'has until now most prominently been employed in the limited sense of describing avoidance of law and moreover seems not to have been generally accepted'. It is a remarkable admission. The first of these points does not provide much support for the need of the concept, since law-avoidance can certainly be disallowed as such without speaking of abuse of right. The second is plainly fatal to the notion that any principle of abuse of right is part of Swedish law.

The author nevertheless writes of a 'growing tendency', which he contends is manifest in four cases decided between 1981 and 2002. Not only does this seem a meagre harvest, but an examination of the cited cases is unpersuasive. In one case the argument was made but not accepted. Another citation was to the individual opinion of a judge, and thus not part of the judgment itself. Yet a third instance concerned the abusive call of an on-demand guarantee; that decision explicitly referred to a case from England (where the doctrine of abuse of right is *not* a part of the law) as persuasive support for the unsurprising idea that payment will not be ordered in 'clear cases of fraud'.

---

[11] J. Munukka, 'Rättsmissbruk – En rättsfigur under framväxt', in M. Schultz (ed.), *Stockholm Centre for Commercial Law Årsbok* (Iustus Förlag, 2008), 135–64.

The demonstration is not assisted by a last, complicated German case that, in the end, seems to have involved an unremarkable rejection on factual grounds of a failure-of-mitigation defence under an insurance contract. The author notes one scholar's expression of doubt that even the 'intention to cause harm' moves the boundary between permitted and forbidden conduct; admits that a similar function is ascribed by Swedish courts to the duty to abstain from chicanery (perhaps borrowed from a well-known article of the German Civil Code) and the duty of 'loyalty' in contractual relations; and finally writes as follows, while acknowledging that this criticism borrows from Planiol's famous, century-old aphorism *le droit cesse, là où l'abus commence* (already translated previously): 'When an abuse of right is invoked, it might be objected that the entitlement relied upon does not extend as far as it has been taken. This would thus not involve a misuse of a right, since the conduct does not actually correspond to an entitlement.'[12]

If this means that there was something of a hiccup in the progress of this doctrine in Swedish law, perhaps some reassurance could be gained by looking at the result of the great work of a multitude of scholars that resulted in the UNIDROIT Principles of International Commercial Contracts. Their goal was to distil general principles with such a degree of confidence that UNIDROIT explicitly invites parties to international contracts to use its Principles as the applicable substantive law of their agreements. It is natural therefore to consult the massive *Oxford Commentary* on the Principles, the second edition of which has grown to comprise no less than 1,528 pages, including a very extensive index.[13] There perhaps would be a treasure trove of references to abuse of right.

Alas, no – and not because the expression was overlooked. In fact, there is one single reference to it, included to explain why 'abuse of right' was *not adopted* as part of the Principles.[14] The editor opines that 'the practical results reached by employing a separate doctrine do not differ'[15] from those produced under the general terms of Article 1.7, which provides: 'Each party must act in accordance with good faith and fair dealing in international trade.' This is plainly a broader formulation than

[12] Munukka, 'Rättsmissbruk', p. 162.
[13] S. Vogenauer (ed.), *Commentary on the UNIDROIT Principles of International Commercial Contracts (PICC)*, 2nd ed. (Oxford University Press, 2015).
[14] Vogenauer, *Commentary on the UNIDROIT Principles of International Commercial Contracts (PICC)*, p. 221.
[15] Vogenauer, *Commentary on the UNIDROIT Principles of International Commercial Contracts (PICC)*, p. 222.

that of the famous and much-copied Article 1134 of the French Civil Code, which specifically relates to the *performance* of contracts (see Chapter 2). Article 1.7 has been criticised by well-known commentators. Jan Dalhuisen has written that it is 'in its generality an inexplicable provision'.[16] Pierre Mayer complains that its 'fuzziness' is likely to be an obstacle to its use as part of *lex mercatoria*.[17] In the first edition of the *Commentary*,[18] the co-editors at that time acknowledged that the content of Article 1.7 is unlikely to be elucidated by reference to the experience of national systems applying standards of good faith, since it seeks to establish 'an autonomous and international standard . . . [and] national standards are largely irrelevant'.[19]

If one doubts that Article 1.7 by itself could be enough for courts or tribunals to infer specific rules of decision, one might go further and look at the Official Comment, since it actually employs the expression 'abuse of right'. The Comment, in fact, contends that Article 1.7 should be understood as capturing abuse of rights when one faces 'a party's malicious behaviour which occurs for instance when a party exercises a right merely to damage the other party or for a purpose other than the one for which it had been granted, or when the exercise of the right is disproportionate to the originally intended result'.

That we reject 'malicious behaviour' defined ('for instance') as amounting to 'abuse' is obvious from the moral judgment implicit in the expression. It is natural to refer to the general concept of 'abuse' as part of the notion that 'abuse of right' should not be allowed, but that does not mean that any of these examples are instances of 'abuse of right'. When specific legislation defines certain conduct as 'abusive' and therefore falling outside the entitlement created by a particular right, the conduct in question will not be an abuse of right for the simple reason

---

[16] J. H. Dalhuisen, *Dalhuisen on Transnational and Comparative Commercial, Financial and Trade Law*, 3rd ed. (Hart Publishing, 2007), p. 297.

[17] P. Mayer, 'Le Principe de bonne foi devant les arbitres du commerce international', in C. Dominicè (ed.), *Études de droit international en l'honneur de Pierre Lalive* (Helbing & Lichtenhahn, 1993), p. 543, see pp. 550–3.

[18] S. Vogenauer and J. Kleinheisterkamp (eds.), *Commentary on the UNIDROIT Principles of International Commercial Contracts (PICC)*, 1st ed. (Oxford University Press, 2007).

[19] Vogenauer and Kleinheisterkamp, *Commentary on the UNIDROIT Principles of International Commercial Contracts (PICC)*, pp. 171–2. The second edition of the *Commentary*, edited by Vogenauer alone, deals with abuse of rights in only two paragraphs (Vogenauer, *Commentary on the UNIDROIT Principles of International Commercial Contracts*, pp. 210–20) and omits, without explanation, the just-cited references to Dalhuisen and Mayer.

that the very definition of the right in question excludes it. Any attempt to impose specific outcomes with respect to conduct that has not received such legislative attention has, to continue the French example, led to a state of affairs where the current edition of the standard French legal reference work *Encyclopédie Dalloz*, under the rubric 'Abus de droit', effectively abandons any quest to furnish a rule or a principle and instead concludes as follows: 'Is it still possible to set out a general theory of abuse of right? The attempt may seem presumptuous; its domain has been so enlarged, its sources so diverse, its criterion so unglued, that it seems hazardous to wish to reconstitute this fragmented subject.'[20]

The reference to 'enlarged domain' is obviously to the omnipresence of the explicit prohibition of specific types of abuse, and not to any 'general principle' – obvious, that is, because the authors of the *Encyclopédie* feel unable to articulate such a principle. Yet Jean-Daniel Roulet identified France as the leading jurisdiction among those he classified as having a 'broad' conception of abuse of right.[21] He considered Germany as the leader within the second category, characterised by a 'limited' conception, and Italy and England as 'opposed' to the theory. One must conclude that the ground for the emergence of abuse of rights as a reliable general principle of international law is hardly fertile.

The reality, like it or not, is that abuse of rights is far from established as a general principle even in national law. The law of any jurisdiction is likely to be filled with definitions of the specific consequences of wrong-doing and abuse, but that does not make either of them a principle. For example, the law of France abounds with references to abuse, whether in Codes (other than the *Code civil* itself, which does not speak of *abus de droit*) or in statutes. For example, the *Code de la famille* speaks of abuse of the right to object to adoption, the *Code des Impôts* of abusive business transactions designed solely to reduce tax, the *Code du travail* of abusive and discriminatory dismissal, and naturally the *Code de Procédure Civile* of abuse of process. Statutes regulate instances of abuse with respect to employment relations, residential leases, intellectual property, unfair contract terms in consumer transactions, and (of course) regulations

---

[20] 'Est-il encore possible de dresser une théorie générale de l'abus de droit? Le projet peut paraître présomptueux: son domaine s'est tellement élargi, ses sources se sont tellement diversifiées, son critère s'est tellement délité, qu'il semble aventureux de vouloir recomposer de façon cohérente cette matière émiettée', L. Cadiet and P. le Tourneau, 'Abus de droit', *Répertoire de droit civil* (Dalloz, 2015; updated in 2017), para. 7.
[21] Roulet, *Le caractère artificiel de la théorie de l'abus de droit en droit international public*, extract reproduced in Chapter 2, note 11.

pertaining to judicial proceedings. All of these texts contain detailed definitions that allow judges to make predictable and context-specific decisions. They do not consist of a single page with the single line *judges will apply the principle of abuse of rights*, which would be more or less another version of *judges will know it when they see it* – a blank check, the abandonment of principle.

The fourth (and only useful) meaning of abuse of rights thus comes to the fore when the law-maker has decided that the potential for mischief with respect to a particular right is so unpredictable that it is best to give explicit discretion to the adjudicator to determine whether a party invoking the right is acting legitimately. A recurrent illustration relates to taxation, and the tendency of some taxpayers to create complicated transactions and structures to seek to rely on a right to a deduction, a credit, or an exemption, although the stratagems employed have no purpose but to avoid taxes. In such cases, the tax courts may be given explicit authority to disregard the scheme, to recharacterise the transaction, and to issue a tax bill on account of an abuse of right. But the otherwise pointless transaction is not illegal per se, and is therefore abusive only because an explicit law or rule deems it to be so. What is needed is a *lex specialis*, not a problematic general principle.

Abuse of *Law* Distinguished

We have already seen that the French and German languages conflate 'the law' and 'a right' in the words *droit* and *Recht*. English allows greater precision, and indeed demands it. French and German speakers are so used to the dual meanings that they easily perceive the meaning intended in a particular context, but English speakers will not say 'you have no law to do that to me' or 'there ought to be a right against that kind of behaviour'.

This distinction is important to the main thesis of this book, which opposes the elevation of abuse of rights to a general principle of law, but takes no issue with the fact that laws should not be abused and that *the law-maker* does well, whenever experience shows it to be useful or indeed necessary, to identify its abuse with contextual specificity and to forbid it.

Rights may of course arise from fundamental but abstract principles such as constitutional promises of due process. Constellations of well-settled meanings may crystallise around such core concepts, but principles invested with the high authority of a constitution, intended to resonate everywhere, should not be numerous, lest they become accessible only to specialists. When the law becomes dominated by areas incomprehensible to anyone but high priests speaking in a rarefied language, the subjects of the law become estranged from it with profoundly deleterious consequences. Rights are better created by specific legislation that involve practical arrangements for life in society: invented, implemented, and reformed in ways that do not implicate such abstractions. A *lex specialis* may be abused in ways which are appropriately assessed by specific analysis of the objectives and concrete context that was the *raison d'être* of that legislation.

To return to the example of taxation: fiscal regulations are often highly technical, involving a combination of political negotiations and technical devices for enhancing public revenues and creating incentives for desirable behaviour. Such laws and regulations, often amended, by and large do not lend themselves to assessments in terms of high-level principles. Yet their abuse is a matter of concern, and dealt with in a targeted fashion. Tax courts in the United States have, since the landmark case of *Gregory* v. *Helvering*,[22] developed a rich jurisprudence that strike down avoidance schemes involving the structuring of economic transactions in ways that have no substantial business purpose, applying the doctrine of substance over form to a multitude of possible transactions in such a way as to create a complex body of learning which becomes the stock in trade of specialists. In France, there is a special *Comité de l'abus de droit fiscal* that decides challenges by taxpayers who feel that the revenue services have wrongly disallowed their 'tax-efficient' transactions as devoid of any purpose but avoidance. Such cases, needless to say, do not call for expertise in legal philosophy, but in the very specific application of technical regulations and precedents, often by specialised courts.

In the international realm, the complex challenges of competing – if not colliding – sovereignty exacerbate the difficulty of establishing a workable unitary definition of abuse of rights. Consider the territorial sea as it was perceived in times past. Assume that all nations agreed that it extended three nautical miles from the coast (the imaginary reach of a cannon shot), and that therefore the coastal state may regulate fishing as it sees fit. What was one to do in a situation of two opposite coasts separated by less than six miles of water? What if each state purported to prohibit fishing by foreigners in their waters? Negotiated adjustments must be brought about. They perforce encroach on sovereignty; the scope

---

[22] *Gregory* v. *Helvering*, 293 U.S. 465 (1935).

for its unilateral exercise is thus ever narrowing. And so we have a Convention on the Law of the Sea.

The so-called *Lotus* principle, inferred from a judgment of the Permanent Court of International Justice in 1927,[23] to the effect that in the absence of an explicit prohibition of international law states have the sovereign authority to act as they see fit, is now broadly discredited because of the realities of the modern world. The fields of exercise of sovereignty overlap in a continuously expanding manner unimaginable just a few generations ago. Adjustments must be made to resolve competing claims. This process may limit each right without any provocative suggestion that either has been abused. In our times, it seems unnecessary to fulminate against the *Lotus* concept. The predominance of *lex specialis* is the price of indispensable (and invaluable) cooperation.

With respect to such necessary international arrangements, the need to contain abuse of their disposition *expands upward* as a rule developed from familiarity with a particular context that requires regulation to ensure international cooperation – *not downward* from the nebulous notion of abuse of rights. Of course it may be said that the arrangements devised reflect a general preoccupation with the need to prevent abuse, but that is obvious to the point of platitude; the general notion is simply not capable, by some feat of uninformed intuition, to produce a solution perfectly fitted – *mirabile dictu!* – to the regulation at hand.

For this reason, one of the criteria offered with some frequency for the finding of abuse of rights, namely *exercising a right in a manner which does not conform to the purposes for which the right exists*, is inapt. Such conduct does not justify the application of the general notion as such. It rather explains the need for specific legislative or judicial countermeasures against unintended and deleterious use of specific laws.

Against this background, it is a matter of concern to see publications like the book *Prohibition of Abuse of Law: A New General Principle of EU Law?*,[24] containing twenty-six written contributions that emerged from a symposium organised by the Center for Business Taxation and the Institute of European and Comparative Law at Oxford, of which twenty-one titles referred to 'abuse of law' and five to 'abuse of rights'. (The introduction by Rita de la Feria, a tax specialist, is headed 'Introducing the Principle of Abuse of Law'.) The foreword, by a former Advocate-

---

[23] *The Case of the S.S. Lotus (France v. Turkey)*, judgment, 7 September 1927, *P.C.I.J.* Ser. A, No. 10.

[24] R. de la Feria and S. Vogenauer (eds.), *Prohibition of Abuse of Law: A New General Principle of EU Law* (Hart Publishing, 2011).

General of the European Court of Justice, speaks of 'the principle of abuse of rights and/or abuse of law' and contends that 'several recent high profile cases' at that Court have transformed the 'principle' into 'one of the most discussed and relevant current issues of EU law'. This collection of essays will be used as a final focal point when exploring the themes of the concluding Chapter 8.

'Abuse of rights' cannot be defined without using open-textured formulations which impede predictability. Bin Cheng did not call abuse of rights a principle, but a theory. In his laudatory preface of Jean-David Roulet's comprehensive rejection of the notion that it could serve as a rule of international law, Cheng in fact declined to take a position as to 'the place of the theory in international law'. Among national legal systems, the most notable movement to establish a principle of abuse of rights (expressed nowhere in the French Civil Code) arose in France at the end of the nineteenth century. It was, and remains, controversial. The common law has found ways to place limitations on the attempted exercise of rights without using the generic reference to abuse as a rule of decision. Conceptually, the notion of abuse of rights is not a necessary corollary to that of good faith.

2

An Idealistic but Troublesome Impulse

We may romanticise the self-reliant independence of the hunter-gatherers and subsistence farmers of distant ancestral times, when each individual knew how to do everything and relied on no one else. But life was nasty, brutish, and short.

We moderns live in crowded environments where our daily lives involve a myriad legal relations, with public authorities as well as with fellow citizens, which continuously affect our conduct. Individuals can prosper, even if they are able to do only one thing; the economic systems that sustain us are based on forms of cooperation that allow such specialisation. Successful modern states benefit from public investments paid for by taxes collected without the use of force.

Social interdependence is a great achievement, and so is the rule of law. Unlike our wild forebears, we expect a nurturing, protective environment. Why, then, should the law not require us to be civil? We are not cavemen, the law not a bludgeon. Rights emerge from the institutions designed for us to live in society; why should their exercise not be conditioned on community values such as solidarity and fair dealing?

Put another way: since the rule of law is bestowed on individuals by society, and cannot be imagined otherwise, how could an antisocial use of the law be tolerated?

Noble Sentiments Are Not Good Rules

One can readily understand the generous impulse that flows from the observation that since unscrupulous individuals are tempted to take advantage of the law to protect unsocial conduct, it is necessary to stop them. One can also understand the attraction of an overarching general principle forbidding what may be convenient to depict, with a very broad brush, as the abuse of rights. Some lawyers operating in domestic settings propagate an untutored conclusion that the notion of abuse of right has given rise to established rules of jurisprudence, and that where this is not so it should be encouraged. (Such thinking, it seems, is seldom promoted by *judges*, even though their authority would be aggrandized by such a development.[1]) Influenced by such voices, many others unthinkingly invoke the putative principle in all sorts of circumstances, more or less to identify and condemn 'conduct I do not like'.

It is possible that the phrase might have the status of a useful rule of decision in a particular domestic legal system. That, however, requires stable and well-understood criteria. Judging by the experience of national courts, such an achievement is rare. It would doubtless require that the system is blessed with a trusted and homogenous judiciary endowed with exemplary legal training and culture. In the international domain, this seems impossible given the heterogeneity of national legal systems.

The concept has been formulated in many more or less intelligible phrases, but perhaps best captured by focusing on its function rather than its moral justification. There seems to be broad agreement that it should be brought to the fore only at the margins of the law, when the rules of law are not equal to the task of dealing with unexpected mischief. The Greco-American scholar Athanassios Yiannopoulus an influential commentator on Civil Code of his adopted State of Louisiana (as a professor of comparative law at the University of Tulane), encapsulated the matter as follows:

> In its function as a corrective device, the doctrine of abuse of right presupposes the existence of a right that that may properly be exercised only within certain bounds prescribed by law. When such bounds are not prescribed by express provision of law, they must be determined by the courts case by case in light of a number of factors, including the presence or absence of intent to harm, the existence or lack of serious legitimate interest,

---

[1] See the observations of Jean Fourré in Chapter 6, note 2.

good faith or bad faith, and consideration of the purpose for which a right is recognized by the law.[2]

This well-crafted summation exposes not only noble intentions but a number of serious difficulties that will be revisited on more than one occasion in this book: (1) if the 'bounds' are 'prescribed by express provision of the law', we must refer to that provision and would create nothing but confusion by speaking of the abuse of rights, since the crossing of bounds means that the right is not secured in the first place; (2) expressions like 'in light of', 'serious', and 'consideration' suggest flexible options rather than rules; (3) in the absence of an explicit legal rule, any decision that requires taking a view on the 'purposes' of laws is likely to be idiosyncratic if not arbitrary; (4) if a rule is intentionally worded in expansive terms, so as to be adaptable to the unexpected, and thus to fulfil a residual function, it seems unavoidable that lawyers will be tempted instead to push it centre stage; and, (5) the pregnant word 'including' reveals that we are far from a definitive formulation, and are perhaps never intended to reach it.

Hohfeld's famous attempt to develop a precise comprehension of the word 'right' grew out of his observation that even eminent scholars use it indiscriminately, so that its meaning may change several times in a single sentence. He proposed a definitional system that would in particular elucidate the distinctions between 'rights', 'privileges', 'powers', and 'immunities'.[3] Hohfeld's project need not detain us for present purposes, save to observe that each of these words is equally problematic if we put the words 'abuse of' in front of them. The *privilege* to enter the royal gardens (which per Hohfeld means that no one has a right to prevent its enjoyment) simply vanishes if its limits are not respected; to race motor cars there is unlikely to be part of the privilege, and there is then no need to speak of its abuse. An *excess of power* is not an abuse of the power because at the point of transgression, the power has simply been lost. And so it is with the usurper of *immunity* who may be guilty of fraud or deception but cannot be said to have abused a status he never had in the first place.

Unsurprisingly, terminological quandaries abound when one seeks to discern legal principles as reflections of a common understanding across linguistic barriers. To take the most salient incongruity: understanding that 'abuse of right' and 'abuse of the law' are not equivalent, what are we

---

[2] A. N. Yiannopoulus, 'Civil Liability for Abuse of Right: Something Old, Something New . . .', 54 *Louisiana Law Review* (1994), 1173, at 1195–6.

[3] W. N. Hohfeld, *Fundamental Legal Conceptions as Applied in Legal Reasoning and Other Legal Essays* (Yale University Press, 1919).

to make of *abus de droit*, since in French *le droit* is 'the law' while *un droit* is 'an entitlement'?

To be sure, the notion that abuse of right should be impermissible is irresistibly appealing as a general proposition. It is more than obvious – indeed a tautology – that law's purposes should not be defeated by allowing rights to be used in ways that would result in injustice or harm the public interest. Having readily accepted this premise, however, we confront the important choice that is the essential concern of this book. On the one hand, should we simply state as a general rule that 'judges may not allow the abusive reliance on any rights', and count on the decision-maker to decide, in any given case, what the word 'abusive' means? Or should we, to the contrary, perceive that the infinite variety of rights means that the definition of their abuse is best left to be a part of the design of the particular right in question, and thus a matter for the law-maker? The latter approach is surely a better way to determine specific and predictable limitations.

Before looking at the unsuccessful efforts in France at the end of the nineteenth century to turn abuse of right into a central tenet of jurisprudence (immediately resisted even there), we should understand that Bin Cheng did not endorse abuse of right as a general principle.

Reading Bin Cheng Properly

Cheng's *General Principles*, published in 1953, was apparently extraordinarily well timed and has remained continuously in print. It is not in essence an analytical work, but rather a distillation of cases in which the author sought to identify a number of 'general principles' applied by international adjudicatory bodies. Lawyers in international practice are familiar with Cheng's useful list, but wonder about things such as whether it misses some concepts that merit inclusion, or was too quick to promote others, and exactly how new principles may emerge.

'Abuse of rights' is indeed there, but only as a *subtitle* of chapter 4, which is actually called 'Good Faith in the Exercise of Rights'. The two notions overlap but are neither synonyms nor mirror images. The good faith performance of contracts is known, it seems, to all systems of law, although under a great variety of terms; the Germans require conduct *nach Treu und Glaube* and the English speak of *implied terms*. The famous Article 1134 of the Napoleonic Civil Code, copied all over Latin America and Francophone Africa, requires that contracts *doivent être éxécutes de bonne foi* (should be performed in good faith).

This means, notably, as Article 1135 makes clear, that contracts require not only the performance of explicitly defined obligations, but also what is called for 'by equity, usage, or law'. *Abus de droit* is nowhere to be seen. When the French speak of 'abusive clauses' in reference to Article 1135, they condemn things like unusual (if not illegal) limitation of liability clauses. In other words, the point is to secure enforcement of contractual duties, *not to define abusive claims of contractual rights.*[4]

We are still at a level of considerable generality. But we can readily see that the good faith performance of agreements is a requirement of positive obligation, whereas the notion of 'abuse of rights' is one of a restriction of rights. It is well worth noting that the Cheng's subtitle is in fact this: '(The *Theory* of Abuse of Rights)'; its parenthetical appearance confirms its tentative status.

The little section devoted to abuse of right is disappointing. One cannot fault the author for failing to describe things he has not seen (i.e., outcomes explicable only by recognition of abuse of right as a rule of decision). One might regret his failure to develop concrete criteria to help lawyers evaluate whether fact patterns may be said to reveal the abuse of rights. Indeed, the qualification contained in its very title suggests a failure to achieve the author's self-assigned task to identify principles 'as Applied by International Tribunals'.

In sum, the status of the 'theory' or 'doctrine' of abuse of right as a general principle seems dubious at the outset. Established general principles have solid foundations in the major national legal systems of law. How otherwise could they be deemed of general applicability in the international community? Abuse of right, on the other hand, is wholly unfamiliar to common lawyers, who have difficulty understanding how a right can be abused. Either a party has a right or not. If it engages in abusive conduct, it should be unable to establish the right. To reach this sensible result, alternative expressions such as 'unclean hands', 'bad faith', 'waiver', or 'unconscionable bargains' may as well be used. In the context of agreements such as contracts or treaties, an even more prevalent and straightforward way of reaching the same result is to interpret the text so that any right it creates does not extend to such circumstances. I am unaware of any clamours for the common law to fill a supposed void by adopting the concept of 'abuse of right'.

Did Cheng somehow find that 'international courts and tribunals' had applied the doctrine as such notwithstanding its lack of antecedents in the common law? It seems not, because if law is to be generated by

---

[4] See the further discussion in the final part of this chapter.

judgments and awards, the most fundamental requirement of the rule of precedent is that the essential *ratio decidendi* of a court or tribunal is precisely the rule being claimed to have the force of law. What one finds instead in *General Principles* are three types of examples:

1. Cases which did not need to refer to abuse of right at all. Two examples should suffice. The *Free Zones* case of 1932 between France and Switzerland involved a treaty obligation to maintain duty-free zones on the mutual border.[5] France nonetheless erected police cordons for other purposes. The judgment observed that France had a right to do so, but not if it *abused* that right to evade the treaty obligation. The same outcome could obviously have been achieved in a more straightforward fashion by holding that the police activity contravened treaty obligations if they had the effect of undermining the treaty. The second case is *Chorzów Factory*, which inter alia concerned Germany's right to alienate property during the period between the signature and the effective date of the Treaty of Versailles.[6] The PCIJ stated that only a 'misuse' of the right would invalidate the act of alienation. This is an equally thin thread on which to hang a general principle of law; no more is really needed to be said than that the Treaty did not forbid alienation prior to the effective date.

2. Cases that referred to the abuse of rights doctrine only by way of an *obiter dictum*, of which Cheng's book provides a characteristically frustrating example.[7] The author asserts that 'the principle of good faith requires a party to refrain from abusing such rights as are conferred to it by a treaty'. Here is exactly where we would like to find evidence of such a rule, since this book is in essence a digest of cases. This phrase is indeed followed by a footnote. But the note consists of nothing more than this high-sounding but unhelpful observation found in the venerable *Sartori* award rendered in 1863: 'The honour and interests of the two republics represented in the joint commission require them to give proof of the good faith with which each of the two countries fulfills the stipulations of the public treaty which binds them and requires that neither government shall allow the citizens so to abuse the protection and guarantees conceded to

---

[5] *Case of the Free Zones of Upper Savoy and the District of Gex (France v. Switzerland)*, judgment, 7 June 1932, *P.C.I.J.* Ser.A/B, No. 46.

[6] *Case concerning the Factory at Chorzów (Germany v. Poland)*, jurisdiction, judgment, 26 July 1927, *P.C.I.J.* Ser.A, No. 9.

[7] B. Cheng, *General Principles of Law as Applied by International Courts and Tribunals* (Cambridge University Press, 1953; paperback, 2006), p. 119.

them by the treaty as to consider them a species of immunity under which they may infringe the laws.'[8]

3. Cases holding that the facts in question did not amount to an abuse of right. (*Chorzów Factory* may be cited again as an example.) That really will not do. Finding that a rule *does not* apply in a given case simply does not create a precedent; it is by definition not the *ratio decidendi*.

When a continental (Swiss) scholar, Jean-David Roulet, writing in French in 1958, as it were on the heels of Cheng and fully familiar with his book, published an entire monograph on '*la théorie*' of abuse of right in international law, his very title indicated considerable skepticism – *Le caractère artificiel de la théorie de l'abus de droit en droit international public.*[9] His conclusion was a clear rejection of abuse of right as a principle of international law. These are, in my translation, the final passages of his monograph:

> If a certain enthusiasm might possibly have been justified during the first years of the League of Nations, the wariness of international tribunals should, however, with our present advantage of distance, make us prudent. Certainly, if applied with moderation and discernment, the theory of abuse of right might possibly render modest service, for example in creating an obstacle to those who, like Skylock, insist selfishly on claiming rights in all their rigour and severity without any care for the damage they cause to others.
>
> But the advantages that the theory of abuse of right might procure are extremely feeble and in fact, contrary to what is claimed by those who defend it, it is not indispensable in international law. In national law itself, as we have seen in the first pages of this study, abuse of right plays a subsidiary role. This characteristic is accentuated in international law. As Scèrni accepts in the conclusions of his work,[10] it would be to render a poor service to the cause of international law if one were to seek to import such a principle into it, because international law does not at present fulfill the necessary conditions for admission. By reason of the primitive and often imprecise character of the rules of international law, the theory of abuse of right, which is already characterized by considerable elasticity and imprecision, loses all utility in the context of international law. To remedy imprecision by a new imprecision cannot lead to positive results. Another task, admittedly more demanding, is presented to international lawyers: conscious of the imperfections of the system, practitioners and theoreticians should make efforts to develop the existing regulations, and to render it more precise. But the principle of abuse

---

[8] Sartori was a US businessman who complained of his wrongful detention by military forces during a business trip to Peru; his claim was partly upheld. See J. Paulsson, *Denial of Justice in International Law* (Cambridge University Press, 2005), pp. 213–14.

[9] J. D. Roulet, *Le caractère artificiel de la théorie de l'abus de droit en droit international public* (Baconnière Neuchatel, 1958).

[10] The reference is to M. Scèrni, *L'abuso di diritto nei rapport internazionali* (Rome, 1930).

of right would not be of any use to them, and, in the end, I remain persuaded
that without the unfortunate and ambiguous expression abuse of right, this
notion, which even today enjoys excessive and undeserved popularity, would
never have seen the light of day.[11]

It is important to observe that Cheng did not reject Roulet's thesis. To
the contrary, he wrote an admiring foreword to the book in which he
explicitly declined to take a position as to 'the place of the theory of abuse
of rights in international law'.[12]

The least one can say is that as far as proclaimed general principles go, this
one is hard to pin down. Still, however elusive it might be, the words 'abuse
of right' are part of civil lawyers' vocabulary and therefore must mean
something. Is there a core sense so useful, or so compelling, that it should
be deemed a general principle even though it is foreign to the common law?

Equivocal French Intellectual Origins and Claims

Anyone who spends some time looking at French cases to see what they
might mean by *abus de droit* will be disappointed, because the digests,

---

[11] In the original: '*Si un certain enthousiasme se justifiait à la rigeur au cours des prèmieres
années d'existence de la Société des Nations, la méfiance des tribunaux internationaux doit
cependant, avec le recul dont nous bénéficions aujourd'hui, inspirer une certaine prudence.
Certes, appliquée avec modération et discernement, la théorie de l'abus de droit permettrai
éventuellement de rendres quelques modestes services, en barrant notamment la route de
ceux qui, à la manière de Skylock, prétend exercer égoïstement leurs droits dans toute leur
rigeur et leur dureté, sans se soucier des dommages qu'il causent a autri.*
    *Mais les avantages que pourrait procurer la théorie de l'abus de droit sont extrêmement faibles
et en fait, contrairement à ce que prétendent ses défenseurs, elle n'est pas indispensable en droit
des gens. En droit interne déjà, ainsi que nous l'avions vu aux premières pages de cette étude,
l'abus de droit joue un rôle subsidiaire. Ce caratère s'accentue encore en droit international.
Ainsi que l'admet Scerni dans les conclusions de son ouvrage, ce serait rendre un mauvais service
à la cause du droit international que de chercher à y introduire un tel principe, car le droit des
gens ne remplit pas pour l'instant les conditions nécessaires à son admission. En raison du
caractère primitive et souvent imprécis de règles du droit international, la théorie de l'abus de
droit, elle-même caractérisée pas une élasticité et une imprécision considérables, y perd toute son
utilité. Remédier à l'imprécision par une nouvelle imprecision ne peut conduire à des résultats
positifs. Une autre tâche, certes plus ardue, s'offre aux jurists internationaux: conscients des
imperfections du système, practiciens et théoriciens doivent s'efforcer de développer et de préciser
la réglementation déjà existante. Mais le principe de l'abus de droit ne leur serait d'aucun
secours, et, en définitive, nous demeurons persuadés que sans l'expression malheureuse et
ambiguë d'abus de droit, cette notion, qui jouit aujourd'hui encore d'une popularité trop grande
et imméritée, n'aurait jamais vu le jour.*' Roulet, *Le caractère artificiel de la théorie de l'abus de
droit en droit international public*, pp. 149–50.

[12] Roulet, *Le caractère artificiel de la théorie de l'abus de droit en droit international public*,
pp. 7–9.

time and time again, read somewhat like Cheng's chapter 4 – that is to say, illustrations of what are not abuses of right. The occasional instances of sanctions for conduct described by this expression in French cases tend to arise as a result of quarrels between neighbours, where A has sought to use his 'right' of property for the purpose of causing nuisance to B next door, such as constructing a false chimney that deprives his neighbour of light. These are simply *collisions of rights*, where one of them has to yield. If there had been no neighbour, the chimney would not offend anyone's concept of the builder's right.

Late-nineteenth-century France, the environment that produced the Napoleonic Code, was an intellectual incubator of the notion of abuse of right. The reason for this movement was, it seems, a reaction to the Civil Code's seeming exaltation of implacable absolutism, notably in the famous Article 544: 'Property is the right to enjoy and dispose of a thing in the most absolute manner (*de la manière la plus absolue*), as long as the owner's use is not prohibited by laws or regulations.' (It is essential to recall that the expression *abus de droit* does not appear in the French Civil Code.) Given this rigid notion of rights, some evidently thought it advisable to manifest obeisance to the dogma of absolutism while calling on judges to outlaw its abuse, which comes to the same thing as the more straightforward but perhaps more difficult path of advocating the piecemeal recognition, specific to the types of rights involved, of limits to intolerable claims of absolutism.

A famous early judgment was handed down in 1855 by the Court of Appeal of Colmar which held that it was impermissible for a property owner to construct a false chimney for the sole purpose of depriving his neighbour of light, on the basis that the law prohibits 'an action inspired by malevolence, accomplished under the impulse of a *mauvaise passion*, without the justification of any personal utility and resulting in grave prejudice to another'.[13]

The next year the Court of Appeal of Lyon followed suit, ordering payment of damages by a land owner who had carried out excavation works with the sole purpose of diminishing the flow of mineral waters that were the principal element of value of his neighbour's land.[14] Neither this nor the *Colmar* judgment used the expression 'abuse of right'. Indeed, the *Lyon* judgment employed an expression of ordinary good sense, which, as we shall see, resembles the reasoning of courts in

---

[13] II *Dalloz de doctrine, de jurisprudence et de legislation* (1856), pp. 9–19.
[14] II *Dalloz de doctrine, de jurisprudence et de legislation* (1856), p. 199.

common law countries when dealing with such problems: 'the right of property perforce finds a limit in the duty to allow the neighbour also to enjoy his property'.

Five years later came the first explicit judicial endorsement of *abus de droit*, by the Court of St-Etienne in a case that involved identical encroachment by another owner of the mineral waters from the same source. The matter went up to the Court of Cassation, which approved the holding that Article 544 could not protect use that was of no 'personal utility' to the defendant but of 'excessive prejudice to another'.[15]

To complete the picture, in the memorable case known as *Clement-Bayard*, the Court of Cassation upheld a judgment from the Court of Appeal of Amiens against a landowner who had built wooden towers, surmounted by iron pickets, in order to make it impossible for his neighbour to use his land as a landing site for lighter-than-air dirigibles.[16]

Looking back in 1958, Roulet wrote this: 'Having appeared without clamor in the caselaw, the theory of abuse of right was soon to penetrate scholarly commentary, the first of which were published in the beginning of the twentieth century and engendered a controversy which time has not defused.'[17] The foremost of the scholars in question was Louis Josserand, whose monograph *De l'abus de droit* appeared in 1905;[18] Roulet also cites Porcherot, Saleilles, Coroi, Roussel, Campion, and Dabin.[19]

Josserand's idealism was hardly subtle; nor was his certitude of exalted purpose: 'as to the legitimacy of this notion', he wrote in his introduction, 'it is in truth the destiny of law which is in question: the object is to determine whether the law is capable, by an outrageous and draconian interpretation, to shield injustice indefinitely or if it should not reanimate itself, humanize itself profoundly with a breath of equity'.[20]

---

[15] I *Dalloz de doctrine, de jurisprudence et de legislation* (1902), p. 79.

[16] I *Dalloz de doctrine, de jurisprudence et de legislation* (1917), p. 79. This was considered to be something of an extension of the prior cases, since the aim of the guilty saboteur was to force his neighbour to purchase his land at a high price to avoid the impediment; thus the gravamen was not the *purpose* (it is permissible to seek profits) but the *means employed*.

[17] Roulet, *Le caractère artificiel de la théorie de l'abus de droit en droit international public*, p. 16.

[18] L. Josserand, *De l'abus de droit* (Arthur Rousseau, 1905).

[19] Roulet, *Le caractère artificiel de la théorie de l'abus de droit en droit international public*, p. 45, n. 19. Also of interest is an article by J. Charmont, 'L'abus de droit', 1 *Revue trimestrielle de droit* (1902), 113.

[20] Josserand, *De l'abus de droit*, p. 6.

Nor was he shy about the role he assigned to his imaginary adversaries: 'The Anglo-Saxons are profoundly individualistic, in their institutions as in their conduct. If their great philosophers readily exalt the inexorable laws of vigorous competition and natural selection by elimination of the weak, their *jurisconsultes*, with expected symmetry, view rights in a rigorous, indeed pitiless light.' Of the 'Anglo-Saxons' ... great philosophers' he cited only one – none other than Herbert Spencer, celebrated in the mid-nineteenth century as author of the since discredited concept of 'survival of the fittest'. As for the jurists, he mentioned only one name, and it is preposterous: Theodore Roosevelt, the boisterous American president, a law-school dropout whose famous maxim was 'speak softly and carry a big stick'; Josserand referred generically to a collection of Roosevelt's essays, published in French translation under the title *L'idéal americain*.

Although it is thus clear that he was a poor comparatist, Josserand was no gentler with those of his own (unnamed) compatriots who did not share his vision and to whom he therefore assigned the role of guardians of injustice. Leaving aside his rhetorical excesses, it must be said that modern readers of *De l'abus des droit* are likely to feel that Josserand's apparently deeply felt concerns are those of a world long disappeared. He was preoccupied by the notion of absolute rights, and the fact that he saw rights in general as expanding at an alarming rate. We moderns tend not to be troubled by the expansion of individual rights. But our perspective is undoubtedly ahistorical.

There was a time when French lawyers could give legal advice with only one text in front of them – namely the Code. Well into the twentieth century, a familiar joke about the imperiousness of senior *avocats*, sitting at unencumbered desks and asked to justify their advice, would quote them thus: 'On what do I base my opinion? Monsieur, on Articles 1 and following of the *Code civil!*' Today, the industrial scale of legislative production is such that hardly any question can be answered by reference to a short general principle asserted to create 'absolute' rights. Writing as early as in 1947, Justice Felix Frankfurter of the US Supreme Court noted that while 40 per cent of the controversies before that Court in 1875 had involved common law litigation, the share of such cases had dropped 'about to zero'.[21] Modern law-making bodies come up with thousands of pages of regulations at an astonishing pace. Qualifications and limitations

---

[21] F. Frankfurter, 'Some Reflections on the Reading of Statutes', 47 *Columbia Law Review* (1947), 527.

abound. Josserand would not have much to write about, and certainly not in his epistolary tone.

Josserand's idiosyncratic idealism may merit a place in a time capsule, but it is important also to note that it was highly controversial even in his day. Indeed, sharp objections to the notion of abuse of right have been raised ever since the expression began to acquire currency. Most notably, Marcel Planiol, the great expositor of the French Civil Code (which did not then and still does not contain the words *abus de droit*), put it as follows in a phrase that is quoted in practically every writing on the subject of abuse of right: '*le droit cesse ou l'abus commence, et il ne peut pas y avoir "usage abusive" d'un droit quelconque, parce qu'un même acte ne peut pas être à la fois conforme et contraire au droit*'. It deserves to be put in the full context of the two relevant sections of the 1902 edition of Planiol's 1078-page *Traité élémentaire de droit civil*,[22] which in English translation reads as follows (the French words just quoted appear in italics in this translation):

> 870. **Absence of liability for lawful acts.** Since wrongfulness is conduct contrary to the law (illicit), an important consequence follows: if I have the right to do something, I am not at fault for having done it; if I have the right to abstain, I am not at fault for not having acted. Thus I owe nothing to anyone, whatever the harm that my action or inaction may have caused another.
>
> 871. **Abusive use of rights.** Modern scholars and legislators have a contrary tendency to consider that the use of a right may have become an abuse, and therefore be wrongful. Frequent references are made to the abusive use of a right, as if these two words have a clear and definite meaning. But one must not be deceived: *the right ends where the abuse commences, and there can be no 'abusive use' of any right, since the same act cannot at once be in conformity with and contrary to the law.*
>   What has led to this phraseology is the fact that most rights are not absolute; to the contrary they have limits beyond which the holder of the right loses his freedom of action and should be considered as having no right. Thus abuse is the conduct of persons, not when they exercise their rights, but when they exceed their limits. At bottom, there is here a sound idea; it is its formulation which is inexact.

In the subsequent edition of his treatise (appearing only five years later, after the publication of Josserand's book), Planiol added the following important gloss:

---

[22] M. Planiol, *Traité élémentaire de droit civil* (Cotillon F. Pinchon, 1901–2), p. 265.

This new doctrine is based entirely on an insufficiently considered formulation; the phrase 'abusive use of rights' is a logomachy[23], for if I use my right, my act is licit; and when it is illicit it is because I exceed my right and act without right. ... To deny the abusive use of rights is not to endorse the permissibility of the great variety of acts which the courts have prohibited; it is only to observe that every abusive act, simply because it is illicit, is not the exercise of a right, and that the abuse of rights does not constitute a distinct juridical category of illicit acts.[24]

Herein lies an essential point; Planiol was not quarrelling with the *outcome* of the judgments that purported to follow this 'new doctrine', but with the invention of an unnecessary purported 'distinct juridical category of illicit acts'. In 1907, automobiles had already appeared on the roads of France, and Planiol observed that promoters of the 'new doctrine' suggested that excessive speed on the part of their drivers should be forbidden as an abuse of right: presumably of the right to own a dangerous contraption, or to use public roads.[25] His reluctance to employ the notion of an abuse of right of course did not mean that he condoned dangerous driving.

Why would it not be enough to say that the defendant simply did not have the right to act as he did, rather than that he was abusing his right as a property owner? All that is required is to see that property rights are not absolute – which is unlikely to surprise any ordinary modern citizen.[26] If he had been able to see it in a crystal ball, Planiol would likely have approved of how the Supreme Court of the State of Idaho handled a similar matter in 1973,[27] reasoning simply that unless a right is absolute it is unavailable when its limits are exceeded, and thus resolved the following problem without needing to acknowledge 'a distinct juridical category of illicit rights'.

---

[23] *Logomachie* in French: a flexible derogatory word likely used here in the sense of 'semantic dead end', or perhaps 'oxymoron'.

[24] M. Planiol, *Traité élémentaire de droit civil* (Librarie générale de droit et de jurisprudence, 1907), section 871. Robert Kolb has recently sought to refute this famous passage. His critique is in turn challenged in the third part of Chapter 7.

[25] Planiol, *Traité élémentaire de droit civil*, section 285.

[26] Roulet, *Le caractère artificiel de la théorie de l'abus de droit en droit international public*, at p. 18, observed that 'the nature of rights is likely to evolve over time' and rights deemed to be absolute (or *discretionnaires*), like those of land owners, lose that character. (He suggested as a plausible candidate the right of a parent to consent to the marriage of a minor child.) But then he seems to have stumbled, when he proposed that the theory of abuse of rights might come into play once that demotion had occurred. All that needs to be said is that the right is limited in certain situations.

[27] *Sundowner, Inc. v. King*, 509 P. 2d 785 (1973).

A certain Mr Bushnell had sold a motel to Mr and Mrs King, and soon thereafter built a new motel next to it. Relations deteriorated, and the Kings built a structure within two feet of the new building, 85 feet long and 18 feet high. It obstructed 80 per cent of Bushnell's motel, blocking the passage of both air and light. The trial judge found that the structure had no business purpose and had been erected out of spite. He therefore ordered that it be reduced to a maximum height of 6 feet. The question ultimately put to the Supreme Court was whether a 'spite fence' constituted an actionable wrong rather than an owner's 'absolute right to use his property in any manner he desired'. The Court held that 'no property owner has the right to erect and maintain an otherwise useless structure for the sole purpose of injuring his neighbor'. The words 'abuse of right' do not appear in the judgment, nor any attempt to extend the holding to some broader principle.[28]

The abstraction *abuse of right* would be a very poor rule of decision. It is rather the identification of the objective pursued by a rule of decision. Thus the legislated or jurisprudential rule in a given legal system may be that *a right may not be used for the sole purpose of harming another*, and it may very well be explained that its goal is to prevent the abuse of rights. This does not run afoul of Planiol's logical objection, since the rule makes clear that the right stops where a defined abuse (sole purpose to harm) begins. Indeed, it is conceivable that courts in a particular country might use the expression *abuse of right* with a settled understanding that this means no more or less than precisely that a right may not be used for the sole purpose of harming another, and as long as this is consistently followed by the courts with the tacit approval of the legislature, there is nothing to complain about. The trouble is the thought that 'abuse of right' alone can have the stature of 'a distinct juridical category of illicit juridical acts', for, as we shall see in Chapter 3, a multitude of competing formulations have been put forward as providing scope and content of a rule against the abuse of right.

Good judges are reluctant to decide cases by invoking the open-textured phrase 'abuse of right', since abuse is very much in the eye of the beholder and practically any decision that depends on personal inclinations or beliefs are likely to lead to accusations of arbitrariness, and certain to lead to the criticism of unpredictability. Such unwanted

---

[28] The Court deemed the case to be different from another, where the issue was not the erection of a new structure but the presence of a dilapidated house that was not 'maliciously erected' when it was built, thereby engaging in the traditional common law evolution of caselaw by successive distinctions.

judicial authority will inevitably trespass on the terrain of the legislature; the latter would fear that it creates rights only for judges to amend or nullify them in accordance with their personal view of their effect in particular cases.

This is not likely to the path preferred by either law-makers or judges. We do not want judges to decide whether an individual 'deserves' public subsidies on a case-by-case basis; we want specific rules that apply to all similarly situated persons. As noted, the 'right' to create legal entities as vehicles for doing business may find its limits in tax avoidance, such as the disallowance of benefits procured by the artificial structuring of transactions that have 'no business purpose' save the avoidance of taxes. Even that may be too general, and require rulings by the legislature or agencies having a designated rule-making function.

A similar and perhaps even more daunting challenge arises when existing 'rights' are exercised in an evolving context of technological innovation. Freedom of expression and of contract are important rights. But what may be the limits of freedom of expression in the expanding cyberspace? What of the limits of a couple seeking to rely on a contract entered into with a surrogate mother who, in the course of months of pregnancy, develops an emotional bond that she never anticipated? Such questions involve fundamental values of a society, and we are unlikely to want them to be decided in fragmented and inconsistent ways, depending on the vicissitudes of litigation and the attitudes of the particular judge assigned to a given case. This is a legislative function.

Turning back to Bin Cheng and his suggestion that 'the theory' of abuse of right may have a place in considering the effects of the duty of good faith performance of obligations, one is struck by the fact that the most illuminating passage of the entire chapter 4 begins on its very first page. It is, in fact, a quotation from the eleven days of oral argument of Sir Charles Russell as counsel for Great Britain in the *Bering Sea* arbitration of 1893. Russell said that British fishermen were acting within their rights, whereupon the following exchange occurred:

THE PRESIDENT:	Unless done maliciously.
SIR CHARLES RUSSELL:	You are good enough, Mr. President, to antici-pate the very next topic. . . . They have every right to complain . . . if it could be truly asserted that any class or set of men had, for the malicious purpose of injuring the lessees of the Pribilof Islands and not in regard of their own profit and interest and in the exercise of their own supposed

rights, committed a series of acts injurious to the tenants of Pribilof Island, I would agree that that would probably give a cause of action; and, therefore, they have a further right (what I might call the negative right) of being protected against malicious injury.

Cheng immediately drew this conclusion: 'The exercise of a right – or supposed rights, since the right no longer exists – for the sole purpose of causing injury to another is thus prohibited.' He observed that the President of the Tribunal 'entertained no doubt about it' and that counsel to the respondent (seeking to avoid liability) 'was not indisposed to admit it'. Thus the 'Anglo-Saxons' whom Josserand viewed with such uninformed distaste have been able to reject the abusive exercise of rights without using that term (and without offending Planiol's logic).

Yet for more than a century now, non-English writers who wish to paint English law into a corner as an absolutist outlier permitting the outrageously abusive exercise of rights invariably refer to *Bradford v. Pickles,* where Lord Halsbury infamously said this: 'If it was a lawful act, however ill the motive might be, he had a right to do it. If it was an unlawful act, however good his motive might be, he would have had no right to do it.'[29]

It is high time to forget this striking sentence, which tells us little about actual decisions, then or now. Court judgments are often criticised in all free societies, and there was certainly a time when English scholars found the common law to be far too harsh.[30] But the common law is not immutable, as this passage from Tony Weir's monograph on the English law of torts makes clear:

> As to deprivation of water, distinctions are drawn depending on whether it is in a stream or not. If the water is merely percolating through the soil, you have no right to receive it at all: it may be intercepted and abstracted with impunity, as Bradford Corporation found when, with a view to forcing a purchase, Mr Pickles prevented the water under his land from reaching their reservoir. But where water in a defined channel is flowing

---

[29] *Bradford Corp. (or 'Mayor of Bradford') v. Pickles* [1895] AC 587.
[30] One such Englishman was a contemporary of Josserand, namely H. C. Gutteridge, who in a gem-like article, H. C. Gutteridge, 'Abuse of Rights', 5 *Cambridge Law Journal* (1933), 22, gave a sympathetic and well-informed account of his French colleague's work that stands in stark contrast with Josserand's simplistic animadversions against *les Anglo-Saxons.*

through, alongside, or under one's land, one is entitled to receive a reasonable amount from it: to put it another way, upstream occupiers may take only a reasonable amount. A distinction is drawn between abstraction and pollution, for there is liability in polluting even percolating water which a lower occupier would otherwise receive pure.[31]

The passages from the *Bering Sea* arbitration should inspire a further reflection. First, the common law (in its many guises) works hard to develop limitations on the exercise of rights. Second – and this is fatal to the abuse-of-right promoters – it has shown itself capable of limiting the exercise of rights without the assistance of a nebulous catchphrase. Whether the use of this capability may be criticised on occasion as insufficient or incorrect is, of course, another matter – and hardly a greater menace than the unpredictability of the complete individual discretion to know abuse 'when I see it'.

We have no difficulty in deriving by induction a possible rule from the general impetus not to reward abuse – namely, the requirement that the *criticised conduct was motivated either by a strategy of fraudulently evading an obligation or else maliciously causing injury to an innocent party*. It hardly needs to be said that such findings must meet a high standard of proof. But, as we shall see in Chapter 3, this is but one conceivable understanding of the 'rule' against abuse of rights in the great blur of definitions.

Not a Necessary Corollary of Good Faith

Proponents of a rule of abuse of right have insisted that it is inherently and beneficially conjoined with the notion of good faith.[32] Before debating the

---

[31] T. Weir, *An Introduction to Tort Law*, Clarendon Law Series (Oxford University Press, 2006), pp. 154–5, also citing *Cambridge Water Co.* v. *Eastern Counties Leather* [1944] 1 All ER 53.

[32] We have seen at the end of Chapter 1 that the editor of the *Oxford Commentary* on the UNIDROIT Principles asserted confidently, by way of explaining the failure to include abuse of rights as a Principle, that the same 'practical results' are already achieved by these general terms of Article 1.7: 'Each party must act in accordance with good faith and fair dealing in international trade.' Anyone who looks at the alternative formulations of abuse of rights in Chapter 3 should conclude that one really cannot derive meaningful rules of decision from such airy nothings. In 'Tort Roots and the Ramifications of the Obligations Revisions', 32 *Loyola Law Review* (1986), 47, W. T. Tête wrote as follows about the Civil Code of Louisiana, on p. 77: 'The concept of abuse of rights as the converse of good faith preserves the link between our contemporary civil code and the very roots of the Romanist legal tradition. It permits the extension of the concept of "good faith" to permit the cautious recognition of tort duties of result as well as those of due diligence and

conceptual logic of this image of necessary unity, one might well consider that it makes very little difference one way or the other. As we have seen, Bin Cheng spoke of the *principle* of good faith and the *theory* of abuse of right. As he was explicitly following an inductive approach in establishing his conception of the general principles of law,[33] we might infer that his distinction was the simple result of observing that the failure of good faith performance of legal obligations has readily been used as the *ratio decidendi* of international tribunals, while abuse of right has a far less certain foundation. But this difference is hardly accidental and can be attributed to the simple fact that the positive obligation of good faith performance of obligations is more determinate than that of the prohibition against what is somehow to be established as an abuse of right.

For example, the law (whether the code in civil law countries or the caselaw of common law countries) holds that an express obligation to do something carries with it an implied obligation to do what is reasonably necessary to enable that performance; that is the sense of Article 1135 of the French Civil Code, which French lawyers know by heart (as do those of the many countries that have incorporated it in their own codes). Thus, if contractors are not able to open a work site without a municipal permit in their name, they may be held duty bound to procure it even though they did not specifically promise to do so.

Of course, people who perform their obligations in good faith are also likely not to abuse their rights, but there is also no doubt a high correlation between such good behaviour and – to take but three among innumerable possible examples – going out of one's way to help strangers in need, giving comfort and assistance to elderly parents, and never mocking those afflicted with a physical handicap. Such instances of good conduct in society may tend to be duplicated with some consistency, and perhaps also to be disregarded en bloc by some types of misanthrope, but there is no reason to insist that different precepts for decent human relations, although morally of a kind, are conceptually linked for the purposes of legal analysis.

To the contrary, it can create confusion and, worse, lead to imperious but sloppy judicial decisions that ignore contextually appropriate specific rules. Take the case of an employer who has the contractual right to

---

prudence. It seems to provide something of a structure within which the judiciary may make policy decisions and articulate them in terms of the rule of law.' The unwelcome prospect of generalised judicial 'policy decisions' is precisely the reason to discourage this facile equiparation.

[33] See the first part of Chapter 7.

relocate employees to a different place of work. He may have the temptation to transfer an unwanted employee to a place that he knows is unacceptable to the latter (who may be caring for a child or parent who needs to stay near medical facilities) to force the employee to resign. The tactic is, of course, designed to save the expenditure of termination benefits.

If the employer cannot show a legitimate business reason for the reassignment, we know this will not work because it is pretextual. The applicable principle is not an amorphous concept; the specifically relevant legal term is constructive dismissal, and the employee will be given the benefits that accompany wrongful termination. Why should this situation be dealt with by invoking the notion of abuse of right? (And yet this is precisely what some have contended is a proper use of the 'principle' of abuse of rights; see formulation no. 23 in Chapter 3.) The terms of employment must be performed in good faith, and by acting pretextually, the employer has breached the contract and is under the circumstances no longer entitled to invoke the clause on transferability. Why refer to the lofty notion of abuse to defeat a right that has purely and simply been forfeited?

To drive this point home, consider the attempt to invoke the notion of abuse of right against individuals in their dealings with the state. A taxpayer has no personal relationship with the tax collector. If he claims an entitlement to advantages by means of an adventurous interpretation of the tax code, he may be said to making an *abusive* claim, but it is surely an unnecessary stretch to call that the abuse of a *right*; he has no right to the deduction – as simple as that.

There is a purely logical reason not to consider that the prohibition of the abuse of right is an adjunct of good faith. The most common manifestation of a legal requirement of good faith concerns loyalty in the *relations* between two parties. Good faith in the performance of contractual relations is to be required because there is a consensual relationship of trust and therefore one of reliance, if not indeed dependence. The unilateral assertion of a right is quite different, and although it is not 'nice' (indeed antisocial), and therefore reproved like other behaviour that offends our sense of considerate behaviour to others, it is of another genus.

Thirty-four different formulations to define abuse of right can easily be derived from a variety of sources. To distill them into a single, internationally acceptable formulation seems impossible. To content one's self with the words 'abuse of right' on the footing that you know it when you see it is to follow a road to arbitrariness. Abuse of process is sui generis and does not belong in the category of abuse of rights.

3

A Cacophony of Criteria

Is the prohibition of abuse of right – in and of itself, as a simple expression at its inherent level of abstraction and generality – suited for application as a rule of decision? This short chapter shows that this is doubtful as a matter of national law, and wholly unlikely in the international perspective.

Depending on when we first encounter the application of a version of the concept of abuse of right to decide an actual case, we might surmise that the definition of the supposed rule is that *the exercise of a right should be prohibited if:*

1. it is abusive (a circular criterion; often disguised by the invocation of lofty purposes),
2. its exercise is 'antisocial',[1]
3. its exercise 'exceeds normal limits',[2]

---

[1] This would seem to suit the purposes of any totalitarian regime irrespective of ideology, but in fact is also found in Article 7(2) of the Civil Code of modern democratic Spain, and in Japan the Supreme Court has pronounced itself (in a case involving a neighbour's complaint that the addition of a second floor to a single-storey house impeded sunlight and ventilation) as follows: 'In all cases a right must be exercised in such a fashion that the result of the exercise remains within a scope judged reasonable in the light of the prevailing social conscience. When a conduct by one who purports to have a right to do so fails to show social reasonableness and when the consequential damages to others exceed the limit which is generally supposed to be borne in the social life, we must say that the exercise of the right is no longer within its permissible scope. Thus, the person who exercises his right in such a fashion shall be held liable because his conduct constitutes an abuse of right.' See Supreme Court of Japan, judgment, 27 June 1972, 26 *Saiko Saibansho minji hanreishu* 1067 (as translated in K. Sono and Y. Fujioka, 'The Role of the Abuse of Right Doctrine in Japan', 35 *Louisiana Law Review* (1975), 1037).

[2] This notion suggests that merely *novel* uses of right are forbidden. An interdiction limited to abnormality recurs in a number of laws; e.g., the second sentence of the just-cited Article 7(2) of the Spanish Civil Code: 'Any act or omission which, as a result of the author's

4. its sole *purpose* is to cause harm (a subjective criterion),
5. its 'sole possible *effect* is causing injury to another' (an objective criterion),[3]
6. its 'only effect is to cause harm to another, without benefit to the owner',[4]
7. it is done maliciously so as to injure others (without reference to other purposes),
8. the right is asserted 'in an arbitrary manner in such a way as to inflict an injury to another which cannot be justified by a legitimate consideration of its own advantage',[5]
9. its preponderant purpose is to cause harm (a subjective criterion),
10. it causes more harm to others than benefit to one's self (an objective criterion),
11. it has a disproportionately detrimental effect on another,
12. it is done without due regard for effects on the interests of others,[6]
13. it has 'no other purpose than to damage another person',[7]
14. it is exercised for another purpose than for which it is granted,[8]
15. 'the use of it, given the disparity between the interests which are served by its effectuation and the interests which are damaged as a result thereof, in all reason has to be stopped or postponed',[9]
16. if 'the nature of the right … [is] such that it cannot be abused',[10]

intention, its purpose or the circumstances in which it is performed manifestly exceeds the *normal* limits to exercise a right, with damage to a third party, shall give rise to the corresponding compensation and the adoption of judicial or administrative measures preventing persistence in such abuse'; see also Article 6-1, Luxemburg Civil Code. A draft amendment to the French Civil Code that would have outlawed 'any transgression of the *normal* exercise of a right' was proposed in 1955 but never adopted; see Chapter 4, note 13.

[3] Section 226 of the German Civil Code, referred to as the Prohibition of Chicanery.
[4] Articles 840 and 1912 of the Mexican Federal Civil Code. Notwithstanding this simple formulation, a judgment of 2002 held that actions under Article 1912 require a showing not only of causation and absence of utility for the holder of the right, but also the intention to cause the damage: Thesis Registry No. 186700, Novena Época, Tribunales Colegiados de Circuito, Semanario Judicial de la Federación y su Gaceta, p. 1231.
[5] R. Jennings and A. Watts (eds.), *Oppenheim's International Law*, 9th ed. (Longman, 1992), p. 407.
[6] As the Belgian Supreme Court once put it: 'when faced with different ways of exercising one's right with the same utility, it is impermissible to choose the one which will be harmful to another' (*entre différentes façons d'excercer son droit avec la même utilité, il n'est pas permis de choisir celle qui sera dommageable pour autrui*). See Belgian Court of Cassation, judgment, 12 July 1917, *Pas. Belge*, I, p. 65.
[7] Article 3:13–2, Netherlands Civil Code.
[8] Article 3:13–2, Netherlands Civil Code.
[9] Article 3:13–2, Netherlands Civil Code.
[10] Article 3:13–3, Netherlands Civil Code. Professor Eduard Meijers, commissioned in 1947 to work on a new Civil Code to replace that of 1838, shortly before his death in 1954 produced

17. there is no legitimate reason for doing so,[11]
18. the effect of doing so is at unreasonable variance with initial expectations,[12]
19. it is done 'fictitiously to avoid a legal limitation or obligation',[13]
20. it seeks to take advantage of a mistake (of fact or legal consequence),
21. it has the effect of causing one's own breach of a legal duty,
22. it contributes (depending on the interests involved) to causing or preventing conditions precedent or suspensive conditions,
23. it is used as a means to attain an illegitimate objective (e.g., using an existing option to transfer an employee only because in his circumstances it will cause him to resign),
24. it invokes a *right to refuse* in a manner which is contrary to 'moral rules, good faith, or elementary fairness',[14]
25. there is no 'serious and legitimate interest that is worthy of protection',[15]
26. it is disloyal (without due consideration of the interests of someone to whom a duty of loyalty is owed; e.g., family member, business partner, neighbour),
27. it is disloyal (without due consideration of the interests of others *generally*),

a first instalment that included this very different forerunner: 'A right cannot be abused if its exercise is left completely to the discretion of the right-holder.' Unsurprisingly it did not survive; even American courts reject contractual stipulations purporting to grant 'complete discretion' – for example, in cases of employers who exercise it arbitrarily in determining incentive payments. (See the text following note 25 of this chapter.) That leaves us to ponder the implications of the reference in the final text to the 'nature' of a right. Is it so hard to imagine the abuse of rights once thought to be absolute, such as the right to refuse to enter into a contract, to defend one's land against intrusion, or to revoke a testament? See also formulation no. 3 (and note 3 listed previously).

[11] As one scholar concluded from a review of cases applying the pre-1992 Dutch Civil Code: 'once a reasonable interest is shown for the exercise of the right, and if it is not inspired exclusively by malice, the interests of others may be disregarded'. See C. Brunner, 'Abuse of Rights in Dutch Law', 37 *Louisiana Law Review* (1976–77), 727, at 738.
[12] From the Official Comment to the *UNIDROIT Principles*.
[13] This was the phrasing of the Permanent Court of Justice in the *Free Zones* case – hardly proof of the need for a principle of abuse of rights since the imposition of the so-called police cordon was in that case straightforwardly contrary to France's treaty obligations. See *Case of the Free Zones of Upper Savoy and the District of Gex (France v. Switzerland)*, judgment, 7 June 1932, P.C.I.J. Ser.A/B, No. 46.
[14] *210 Baronne St. Ltd. Partnership v. First Nat'l Bank of Commerce*, 543 So.2d 502, 507 (La. App. 4th Cir. 1989), writ denied, 546 So.2d 1219 (1989).
[15] *210 Baronne St. Ltd. Partnership v. First Nat'l Bank of Commerce*, 543 So.2d 502, 507 (La. App. 4th Cir. 1989), writ denied, 546 So.2d 1219 (1989).

28. the claim of right is stale as a result of the passage of time,[16]
29. it consists of procedural initiatives in connection with legal proceedings that are not permitted under the rules,[17]
30. it 'exceeds the limits imposed by good faith, good customs, or the social or economic purpose of the right',[18]
31. it fulfils *any* one of a selection of the criteria listed previously,
32. it fulfils *every* one of a selection of the criteria listed previously,
33. it fulfils a selection of the criteria listed previously as non-exhaustive examples,
34. a judge or arbitrator declares it to be an abuse of right.[19]

It is essential to understand that this list cannot be consulted and put to use as though one were in a grand emporium, free to pick and choose with the assurance that anything goes because everything is available at the abuse-of-right stall. No – choices must be made, depending on how far the relevant applicable law has gone to make considerate and reasonable behaviour compulsory. For example, proportionality of the benefit of the exercise of the right, as compared to the detriment to the complainant, either is or is not a part of the elements of the rule.

Moreover, each result is likely achievable by the application of other rules. For example, Shakespeare's Merchant of Venice, who threatened to 'exercise' a contractual 'right' to extract a pound of flesh from his defaulting debtor, might be said to have run afoul of formulation no. 2, but why bother? He could not have claimed his right in court because the contractual term was unenforceable; if he had tried to enforce it, he would have been arrested for assault, and had he actually enforced it by self-help, he would have been convicted of murder. To take more realistic situations, there is no need to speak of abuse of rights when the right claimed is, in fact, unenforceable because it involves deceit, intimidation, chicanery, excessive disproportion of bargaining power, unconscionable terms, and an illegitimate or pretextual purpose such as procuring an employee's resignation by instructing him to do things he is unlikely to accept. It is striking, for example, to observe that when the *civil law* courts of Quebec adopted a theory of abuse of right to require reasonable notice

---

[16] Suggested by G. P. Fletcher, 'The Right and the Reasonable', 98 *Harvard Law Review* (1985), 949, at 980.
[17] An obviously redundant rule.
[18] Article 334, Portuguese Civil Code; similarly Article 281, Greek Civil Code; and Article 266, Bolivian Civil Code.
[19] Surely no adjudicator would own up to this formulation, yet this is in effect the 'rule' when abuse of rights is invoked as justification without identifying a more specific criterion.

even in the case of a loan payable 'on demand', several of them invoked
the leading federal Supreme Court case of *Lister* v. *Dunlop*, applying *the
common law* of the Province of Ontario to the effect that such a demand
(i.e., right) may simply not be exercised in the absence of reasonable
notice – which means that there is no logical purpose for speaking of its
abuse.[20]

Not only does the list seem infinitely expansive; it is probably a matter
of controversy (or at least doubt) wherever it is claimed that abuse of
right is an applicable principle. For example, although courts in
Louisiana (the sole civil law jurisdiction in the United States) have
proclaimed the definition of abuse of right in what appears as formulation no. 24, which would seem to put Louisiana in the vanguard of an
extraordinarily amorphous and therefore expansive and unpredictable
adherence of the doctrine, its State Supreme Court has stated the doctrine
should be used only in limited circumstances, given its possible
encroachment on individual rights and obligations.[21]

Formulation no. 29 (which could itself be part of a different list or set
of subcategories) does not belong on this list at all. Misuse or abuse of
process is simply an attempt to employ the mechanisms of the legal
process in ways that are not permitted. Rules to supress abuse of process
are not the creatures of some intuitive application of the notion of abuse
of rights. Vexatious litigation and obstructive procedural tactics are
disallowed because they are disruptive in light of the particular requirements of an orderly disposition of matters before the court, as informed
by the experience of life in court – not because they fall under a sweeping,
undifferentiated category of abuse of rights.

Robert Kolb has addressed this matter, which he calls 'The Prohibition
of Abuse of Procedure', as follows:

> It consists of the use of procedural instruments or rights by one or more
> parties for purposes that are alien to those for which the procedural rights
> were established, especially for a fraudulent, procrastinatory or frivolous
> purpose, for the purpose of causing harm or obtaining an illegitimate

---

[20] See R. Jukier, '*Banque Nationale du Canada* v. *Houle*: Implications of an Expanded
Doctrine of Abuse of Rights in Civilian Contract Law', 37 *McGill Law Journal* (1992),
221, at 231, n. 40.

[21] This led it to reject a claim that an employer had abused the right of termination because it
put an end to a group insurance plan that otherwise would have covered an employee who
became a quadriplegic as a result of a non-work-related injury. *Massachusetts Mutual Life
Ins. Co.* v. *Nails*, 549 So.2d 826 (La. 1989). See the more extensive illustrative discussion of
the law of Louisiana in the third part of Chapter 4.

advantage, for the purpose of reducing or removing the effectiveness of some other available process or for purposes of pure propaganda. To these situations, action with a malevolent intent or with bad faith can be added. The existence of such an abuse is not easily to be assumed; it must be rigorously proven. The concept cannot be caught completely in the abstract, since it can relate to a variety of different situations.

The case law of the ICJ is replete with instances where the principle of abuse of procedure has been invoked. The Court, however, has never found the conditions for an application of the principle to be fulfilled.[22]

This should give pause: there have been many complaints of abuse of process, but not a single one has succeeded. Practitioners should not be surprised. Procedural controversies arise; one side wants to do something which the other finds objectionable; the court rules. It does so in light of its conception of a fair and orderly process; there is no need to speak of abuse, or indeed to define the 'right' that is allegedly being abused. So when a party asks for provisional measures, or for the disclosure of documents, and the other protests that the application is abusive, the court has no need to refer to the 'right' to a provisional measure or a set of documents (in fact, there is only a right to make a *request* to that effect), let alone to the 'right' to a fair trial. It simply decides whether the application is well founded or not. If trial judges consider it vexatious or oppressive or otherwise excessive, they will so rule as a routine matter of procedure.

In a layperson's terms, the submission of forged documents as evidence in court might be thought of as an abuse of the right to be heard in court, but it is more appropriately (and conceptually useful) to be given contextual specificity as a fraud on the court which may have serious consequences for the guilty party – and counsel – apart from its effect on the merits of the dispute.

We certainly would not want to take the road of boundless rhetorical expansion until we reach the point of saying that whatever the judge dislikes is an abuse of 'the right to exist in society'.

It is instructive to study an example of the difficulties encountered by writers tempted by the intuitively compelling force of the expression 'abuse of right' to yield to a Josserandist impulse of exalting it as an overarching rule of decision, ready to fill in when the body of more specific rules does not seem to provide a remedy against an unusual

---

[22] In A. Zimmermann et al. (eds.), *The Statute of the International Court of Justice: A Commentary*, 2nd ed. (Oxford University Press, 2012), p. 904.

kind mischief. We can find one in a lengthy article (sixty pages) published in 1995 by Joseph Perillo, a well-regarded professor at the Fordham Law School best known as co-author of the textbook *Perillo and Calamari on Contracts*, under the title 'Abuse of Rights: A Pervasive Legal Concept'.[23]

The very first paragraph should give pause in two respects. First, Perillo stated his 'thesis' to be 'the existence in American law of a doctrine of "abuse of rights" ... developed ... from its Civil Law analogue' to an extent 'not recognized by American scholars and lawyers'. Yet the existence of a 'doctrine' (or 'concept', to echo the word in his title) is neither revelatory nor controversial. We all know that rights can be abused, and that such conduct should not be allowed. The question should therefore be whether the expression itself can serve as a workable rule of decision (as opposed to a self-evident objective when drafting specific laws).

Eyebrows should also rise when the reader encounters this admission blandly offered in footnote 6: 'Civil Law countries are by no means in accord with one and another with respect to the scope of the doctrine.' That this is an understatement should be clear from the thirty-four formulations set out above, which should be enough to put into question the usefulness and accuracy of referring to 'a pervasive concept' rather than to a variety of manifestations of the rejection of abuse of rights.

Perillo would hardly have contented himself with such an approximation if he was examining US laws or cases. This is the danger with observing that the notion of abuse of rights exists in various foreign jurisdictions, and embracing the abstract expression without concern for the reality that it has failed to generate heterogeneous rules of decision.

Moving to the substantive development of Perillo's article, we find that it consists of an extensive review of instances where US law (including notably caselaw) provides explicit rules for fixing the boundaries for the exercise of rights – for example, abusive discharge of at-will employees, retaliatory termination of contracts, retaliatory eviction, abusive refusal of consent, abusive insurance terminations, abusive acceleration of debt, and abusive calls on demand notes. Two further examples may be noted with further explanation: the US Supreme Court developed the so-called *Noerr-Pennington* doctrine to counter a pattern of oppressive litigation brought by property developers troubled by petitions by aggrieved

---

[23] J. Perillo, 'Abuse of Rights: A Pervasive Legal Concept', 27 *Pacific Law Journal* (1995), 37.

neighbours against the construction of buildings or development of land. Such petitioners were likely to give up rather than to face the high cost of defending all kinds of contrived suits (e.g., claiming defamation, interference with prospective advantage, and the like). The *Noerr-Pennington* doctrine allowed such suits to be dismissed on the grounds that they tended to stifle the exercise of the constitutional right to petition.[24]

Similarly, where bonus payments or the withholding of incentive compensation are contractually defined as being wholly subject to the payor's discretion, some US courts have held that such stipulations nevertheless do not allow arbitrary use of the discretion.[25] Perillo suggests that if a 'concept' of abuse of rights were 'generally adopted', it would be possible to reason under a new framework, for example to inquire as to the purpose of a right and to assess the legitimacy of its exercise in light thereof. Thus, if the purpose of rewarding incentive compensation is found to be 'to instill employee loyalty and act as an incentive to remain' with the employer and 'work harder at assigned tasks', the claim for incentive compensation by an employee *who has resigned* might be rejected; but if the purpose was to withhold earnings until a project is completed, a refusal to pay would be an abuse of discretion under what Perillo referred to as 'abuse of rights analysis'.[26]

None of this requires the adoption of an elusive definition of abuse of right as a rule of decision. What the many instances given by the author show is that the law in the United States has been able to deal with abuses of right in a number of context-specific ways.[27] One might well say, returning to the first paragraph of the article, that the failure of American 'scholars and lawyers' to recognise 'the existence in American law of a doctrine of "abuse of rights"' has not prevented the law from curtailing the abuse of rights, and that the need for a 'pervasive concept' (whatever that might mean) is not established.

---

[24] Perillo, 'Abuse of Rights', 68.
[25] Indeed, the US Uniform Commercial Code provides in Section 1–102(3) 'that the obligations of good faith, diligence, reasonableness and care prescribed by this Act may not be disclaimed by agreement'.
[26] Perillo, 'Abuse of Rights: A Pervasive Legal Concept', 73.
[27] See e.g., J. P. Dawson, 'Duress through Civil Litigation: I', 45 *Michigan Law Review* (1947), 571; J. P. Dawson, 'Duress through Civil Litigation: II', 45 *Michigan Law Review* (1947), 679; J. P. Dawson, 'Economic Duress – An Essay in Perspective', 45 *Michigan Law Review* (1947), 253. Identifying cases constituting duress, the Restatement (Second) of Contracts includes instances where 'what is threatened is otherwise use of a power for illegitimate ends'. See Section 176(2)(c), Restatement (Second) of Contracts (1981).

Infinitely adaptable criteria like those of the first thirty-three of these formulations should frighten anyone who acknowledges the need for discipline and specificity in the articulation and application of rules of decision. But there is, in fact, a far greater danger than this potpourri of things decent people dislike, which at least has the merit of flowing from an impulse to provide a reason for decisions, and that is the thirty-fourth formulation. It fits the *Benetton* case, to be discussed in the next chapter, where French courts plainly seized on the august aura of the phrase *abus de droit* to assume the prerogatives of deciding unprecedented issues of public policy. The reader will be challenged to imagine what 'rule' they were following apart from something like formulation no. 34.

If one insists that abuse of right is a general principle of law, one must also explain how the decision-maker will apply it. Unless it is to be a matter of unlimited discretion (or of 'the length of the Chancellor's foot'[28]), it is indispensable for it to be shored up by a more precise standard: a rule that gives those who are subject to the law a reasonable way to conduct themselves so as to be in compliance, and those who end up in court to argue their cases on something better than guessing at the predispositions of the court or tribunal. Otherwise, to quote the last sentence of Gutteridge's gem-like article eighty years ago:

> However much we may desire to prevent unscrupulous and malignant persons from carrying on their intrigues behind a screen of feigned legality, we may well pause before we give general recognition to a theory which purports to secure an equipoise between rights vested in different persons, but which may in effect be destructive of the liberty of the individual.[29]

But as we shall now see, we seem to be facing a principle in search of a rule, and *unlikely* to be able to generate such a rule with adequate specificity in heterogeneous modern communities. Given that general principles of international law must be distilled from national laws as a synthesis, this failure seems *inevitable* for the international community as a whole.

---

[28] As an English scholar of the law (John Selden) is said to have put it in the 1600s: 'One Chancellor has a long foot, another a short foot, a third an indifferent foot: 'tis the same thing in a Chancellor's conscience.'

[29] H. C. Gutteridge, 'Abuse of Rights', 5 *Cambridge Law Journal* (1933), 22, at 45.

Notwithstanding Josserand's ardent and decades-long exhortations, the theory has remained controversial in France; a proposal in the mid-twentieth century to bring it into the Civil Code was abandoned. The Benetton case offers a troubling illustration of the potential for arbitrariness left in Josserand's wake. Because its courts express themselves in English, Louisiana is a convenient example of the many civil law jurisdictions which pay lip service to abuse of right but scarcely apply it. The common law does just as well without it (as good judges everywhere, unenthusiastic about the expansion of judicial discretion, seem to prefer). The Himpurna case provides an illustration of the unnecessary invocation of abuse of rights.

4

A 'Principle' with No Rules?

The French Evolution

It is instructive to consider the subsequent evolution of the ideas Louis Josserand first presented in *De l'abus des droits* (see the final part of Chapter 2). Published in 1905, this monograph took inspiration from a few French cases dealing with nuisance to property and elaborated a comprehensive theoretical jurisprudence founded on the concept of abuse of right. The little book (eighty-nine pages) is the one traditionally cited by authors reviewing the history of the notion, but it was far from the author's last word on the subject; by 1927, he had expanded his reflections into a 426-page work, mostly forgotten although bearing the portentous title *De l'espirit des droits et de leur relativité: Théorie dite de l'Abus des Droits.*[1]

Josserand believed in the permanent subjection of individual rights to the interests of society; rights are thus always 'relative' to broader concerns about the effects of their exercise on the general welfare. Consequently, the prevention of abuse of rights was a fundamental and perpetual requirement of justice, whatever positive law might say. The failure of this more ambitious opus to secure the universal attention (and adherence) sought by its author goes a long way in explaining the problems of the notion of abuse of right.

De l'espirit des droits carried a message of nearly spiritual fervour delivered in majestic phrases without much apparent interest in analysis or even

---

[1] L. Josserand, *De l'espirit des droits et de leur relativité: Théorie dite de l'Abus des Droits* ('Of the Spirit of Rights and of Their Relativity: The Theory Known as Abuse of Rights') (Librarie Dalloz, 1927).

accuracy. (Recall from Chapter 2 Josserand's castigation of what he viewed as the primitive antisocial attitudes of 'Anglo-Saxon' philosophers and legal scholars, of which his only exemplars were, absurdly, Herbert Spencer and Theodore Roosevelt.) One might have expected that the longer work, with the benefit of more than two decades of further reflection, would be more sober, but that is hardly so. The introduction of the later book consisted of a brief reformulation of his passionate call for the constant presence of a fairer, 'social' vision of the law, and then a series of lengthy and rather repetitive exercises, comprising well over half the book, explaining how this vision would temper the French law in a series of areas: property rights, secured transactions, civil procedure, family law, contracts, individual and corporatist liberties, administrative law, and conflict of laws.

The author continued with a disturbingly superficial eighteen-page review of comparative law, consisting of sketchy impressions of the laws of Germany, Austria, Switzerland, the Soviet Union, Belgium, Italy, Spain, the 'Scandinavian countries', and then two pages on 'Muslim law' in which he speculated that because 'this law is in close contact with morality and religion', the concept of abuse of right 'ought to find . . . an exceptionally favourable environment'.[2]

Then followed three pages on '*les legislations absolutistes*', which is how Josserand categorised the entire common-law world.[3] Once again he casti- gated 'a race which follows the cult of action and men of action', and once again he quoted the same essay by Theodore Roosevelt that he had refer- enced twenty-two years earlier in *De l'abus de droit,* now referring to it disparagingly as a 'replique' to the dictum *suave mari magno* – that is to say, the Roman philosopher Lucretius's way of contrasting those who are secure in the truth of philosophy and those who are not.[4] This was evidence, so he posited, of an 'Anglo-Saxon' position to the effect that a right must be

---

[2] Josserand, *De l'espirit des droits et de leur relativité*, p. 281. In fact, a prominent Libyan lawyer, then living in exile in London, found from his research on the topic that among the scholars of the Sharia, there were 'purists' who would not admit any liability for injury 'arising from the exercise of rights' and 'pragmatists' who would not allow *intentional* injury, 'though arising from the exercise of a recognised right, to escape liability'. He wrote that, in the end, the position remained unsettled: one 'could rightly conclude that the adoption or rejection of the concept has behind it the authority of the Sharia'. See A. Al-Qasem, 'The Unlawful Exercise of Rights in the Civil Codes of the Arab Countries of the Middle East', 39 *International and Comparative Law Quarterly* (1990), 396, at 397.

[3] The third and final part of the 1927 book is an 'essay' on Josserand's theory of abuse of rights as an overriding regulator of the law of rights and liabilities, which essentially echoes and expands upon the author's original treatise.

[4] Josserand, *De l'espirit des droits et de leur relativité*, p. 284, n. 2.

absolute if it is to exist at all. This time he did not refer to Herbert Spencer by name, but he might as well have done so: 'Thus in America as in England . . . it is Darwin's law which . . . ensures the selection of the species by the elimination of the weak.'[5]

There is no evidence in his writings that Josserand was able to consult English-language authorities with any degree of competence, but he nonetheless repeatedly cited the third edition of Frederick Pollock's *Law of Torts* as revealing 'innumerable instances' of 'pitiless . . . nearly prideful' adherence to this 'harsh logic' – in America, it seems he believed, as well as in Pollock's England. One might regret that someone did not supply Josserand with a much simpler book, namely J. K. Mannooch's *Analysis of Sir Frederick Pollock's Law of Torts for Students,* in which passages like this could have caused him to reconsider his harsh and simplistic prejudices:

> What amount of annoyance will amount to nuisance in points of law cannot, by the nature of the question, be defined in precise terms. Where nuisance is once proved, the defendant's intention is immaterial; but a proved intention to annoy may be relevant to show that the defendant was not using his property in an ordinary and legitimate way.[6]

Josserand's remarkable ignorance in this respect need not detain us, except to observe that it illustrates the dangers that arise when writers set out to justify a preconceived conclusion. No reader searching for an analytical demonstration is likely to accept the flowery phraseology of another age as a substitute. What is essential is to realise how far Josserand's fervour took him. On the second page of *De l'espirit des droits*, he wrote this:

> [S]urrounding the formal rule, surrounding the written law, lives an entire percolating world of principles, directives, and standards . . . like a sort of *super-legality.* . . . Although no text of positive law sets them down in a general form, the reality of these customary dogmas, and especially [that of abuse of right], is not only as certain as that of principles enunciated in the most express and imperative terms, but indeed even more certain since their reality escapes the arbitrariness of legislatures which should not be allowed to disregard superior truths of which they are not the creators and to which they are themselves subordinated. . . . The rights created by a legislature do not appear like abstractions in a vacuum; they

---

[5] Josserand, *De l'espirit des droits et de leur relativité*, p. 285.

[6] J. K. Mannooch, *Analysis of Sir Frederick Pollock's Law of Torts for Students*, 3rd ed. (Stevens and Sons, 1920). In all likelihood, Josserand was unacquainted with *Rylands* v. *Fletcher*, the landmark case decided as early as 1868, LR 3 HL 330 (UKHL), by which English tort law was transformed by the holding that a landowner was responsible for the negligence of contractors doing work on his land that caused flooding in an adjacent mine.

operate in and for the social environment; their effect reflects this environment, not by favouring a particular direction but by being attentive to particular objectives; it is their destiny to accomplish justice, and they are incapable of rebelling against justice save at the price of a juridical contradiction, that is to say of an abuse which would merit sanction.[7]

Such lofty collectivist abstractions perhaps would have been suited to the writings of Lenin and others who view laws as subject to the higher aspirations of the collective – as determined by its leaders. But such an acontextual observation is unlikely to be meaningful. (Josserand was born before Lenin and could not have heard of him when he wrote *De l'abus des droits*.) What matters for the purposes of this book is Josserand's implicit – and therefore unexplained but apparently resolute – insistence that law ultimately is to be dispensed by judges and not legislatures, a notion as far as it possibly could be from the mind of Lenin.

Josserand's position seems to have been a reaction to particular developments in French law. In 1937, he published a much-discussed note in a prominent French legal periodical under the title *Sur la reconstitution d'un droit de classe* ('On the Reestablishment of Law Based on Class'), where he detailed the emergence of a series of 'counter-revolutionary' laws regulating commercial, artisanal, rural, medical, and industrial occupations, as well as associations and unions, thus recreating a class society dependent on professional categories. ('Class law is nothing but the projection into law of the battle of classes; its permanent and implacable dynamism makes it an instrument, not of social tranquillity, but of civil war.'[8])

For Josserand, the doctrine of abuse of right not only serves to fill gaps but supplants positive law – to which it is superior. That is startling enough, but there is more. In his chapter on real property rights, he started out by accepting that property rights cannot be and are not

---

[7] Josserand, *De l'espirit des droits et de leur relativité*, p. 2. Again, after a reference on page 4 to the 'triumphal march of the theory of the abuse of right' and an expression of disdain on page 6 for the Napoleonic codification's 'hatred of the past' and its 'exaltation of sacred inalienable individual rights', this remarkable summation appears on page 7: 'In reality, it is not so much as individuals that men are of interest to the law-maker, the public authorities, and the lawyer, but rather as social units; they do not invoke their rights and make them effective in some interplanetary space, but in a social environment of which they constitute innumerable cells, fragile and minuscule; subaltern wheels coupled to a complex and formidable mechanism, they must conduct themselves in accordance with the environment from which they emerge; each time that they exercise a right, be it ever so individualistic and egotistic in appearance, they nevertheless achieve a social prerogative, and it is therefore in a social orientation that they must utilise it, in conformity with the spirit of the institution, and thus civilise it.'

[8] L. Josserand, 'Sur la reconstitution d'un droit de classe', Chron. 1, *Dalloz hebdomadaire* (1937).

absolute; 'salutary, important and numerous' restrictions have been established by statutes, regulations, and case law.[9] They adjust property rights that would otherwise collide. Because these are merely rules to be obeyed, there is no need to refer to the state of mind or subjective intentions of the trespasser. Therefore, 'we are completely outside the domain of abuse of property rights'.[10]

This is a remarkable admission. It seems to concede that the concept of abuse of rights is unnecessary as long as the law steps in to make indispensable regulations. The need for rules of decision has long been clear to the English, whose only fault (in Josserand's perception) seemed to be that they wanted to know where they stood rather than await the opinions of individual judges as to what conduct might fall under the alien abstraction 'abuse of right'. One need only look at a primer on the law of torts to understand the complexity of the challenge and the attentiveness of English law-makers and judges when they deal with the limitations of the rights of property.[11]

That these problems are better dealt with on an ad hoc basis by judges referring only to the phrase 'abuse of right' is a dubious proposition. In any event, Josserand thereafter clarified that he would settle for nothing less than the most extreme form of vindication for his concept; rather than applaud when the legislature or a body of case law defines intolerable types of abuse, he would accept no such satisfaction, given his quest for a more exalted victory: no more nor less than *judicial disregard of law* in order to do justice. Here is what he wrote: '[T]he restrictions placed on land ownership, whether by statute . . . or by caselaw and under the rubric of obligations of *voisinage* [relations among neighbours] invariably fall outside the theory of abuse of property rights, which implies a misuse of the right in a direction other than the one intended by the law, thus violating the institution.'[12]

---

[9] Josserand, 'Sur la reconstitution d'un droit de classe', 14.

[10] Josserand, 'Sur la reconstitution d'un droit de classe', 16.

[11] Chapters 9 and 10, on trespass and nuisance, in T. Weir, *An Introduction to Tort Law*, Clarendon Law Series (Oxford University Press, 2006), should suffice for this purpose. The following passage, on page 158, hardly puts us in the mind of Theodore Roosevelt, Herbert Spencer, or social Darwinism: 'The tort of nuisance would be simpler if it dealt only with disamenity between neighbors, but even then it could not be very simple, because almost anything a neighbor does – cooking exotic foods, playing the trombone, running a school, adding an extension – affects the person next door or above or below him. Yet since he, just like the claimant, is entitled to enjoy his property, there must be some accommodation between a person's right to hold a party and a neighbor's right to sleep undisturbed: both are asserting the same right to sleep undisturbed: both are asserting the same right to enjoy their property.'

[12] Josserand, 'Sur la reconstitution d'un droit de classe', 19.

It is essential to reflect on the extremism of this statement. Instead of taking 'yes' for an answer, Josserand insisted on having it all his way; the 'numerous' laws and regulations that outlaw the abuse of rights – with the effect that the right is simply never established and thus we do not require a doctrine of abuse of rights – made no impression on him. He demanded a principle that trumps positive law – a principle apparently derived from the 'spirit' of law and given concrete meaning by whomever turns out to be the judge of a given case. This seems to reflect a desperate attachment to a legal scholar's version of *l'art pour l'art*.

As it happens, in the beginning of the twentieth century, when *De l'abus des droits* came out, a French commission on the review of the Civil Code, noting the interest generated by court cases limiting the antisocial exercise of rights (notwithstanding the absence of a legislated warrant for doing so), had grappled with the possibility of an amendment to the Code to that effect. The effort was abandoned in 1905. Josserand would have been pleased (if but for a moment) to find it resurrected half a century later, when the commission actually came up with the following proposed wording:

> **Abnormal Exercise of Rights**
>
> Any transgression of the **normal** exercise of a right whether manifested by the **intention** of the actor, by its **object**, or by the **circumstances**, is not protected by the law and may give rise to the actor's liability. This provision does not apply to rights which by their **nature** or under the law may be exercised in a discretionary manner.[13]

Looking at this attempted codification of the concept of abuse of right, one is first struck by the fact that the most attentive legal minds of France could do no better than to come up with a series of abstractions, distilled in the words reproduced in bold in the provided quotation, which would make it exceedingly difficult to predict what the courts might do with a given set of circumstances. Worse, it would leave ordinary citizens shaking their heads in perplexity, since the text required them to understand that a right which 'may be exercised in a discretionary manner' is a so-called absolute right, and then ask themselves if this exception means that *any* exercise of an absolute right is 'normal' (because it is permitted). If so, the second sentence thus defeats the purpose of the evocation of abuse of rights. This seems irremediably disorienting, given

---

[13] Article 147 of a 1955 draft revision of the Civil Code, quoted in J. D. Roulet, *Le caractère artificiel de la théorie de l'abus de droit en droit international public* (Baconnière Neuchatel, 1958), p. 46, n. 28.

that the illustration par excellence of an absolute right was and remained Article 544, concerning the very rights of ownership the courts had limited in cases that gave rise to the movement in the first place (see the third part of Chapter 2).

As one member of the commission pointed out, non-discretionary rights have limits established by law and can therefore, in any event, never be 'abused' because attempts to 'exercise' them beyond those limits are simply contrary to the law.[14] Would one, as Josserand proposed, henceforth have to bear in mind an inchoate category of rights, discretionary or not depending on the evolution of society – involving such things as a woman's right to refuse tutelage, an ascendant's right to oppose the marriage of a descendant minor, or the right to cut roots and branches encroaching on one's land?

A Disturbing Illustration: The French *Benetton* Case

These questions may be left in the ether, because the Civil Code was not amended to refer to (let alone define) abuse of rights. So the music stopped – but the melody lingers on, as from time to time French judges reach into the recesses of their memory to resurrect the phrase *abus de droit* and employ it to justify a particular decision.

Thus in 1995, the *Tribunal de grande instance* of Paris (the civil court of first instance) was seised of a complaint brought against the Italian clothing company Benetton, known at the time for provocative advertising designed to generate attention to its trademark rather than to the design or the qualities of its apparel. One such campaign featured a series of billboards displaying the midsection of a nude human torso upon which the sole letters 'HIV POSITIVE' appeared as a tattoo. (Others used images evoking racism, religious intolerance, violence in Rwanda and former Yugoslavia, and 'boat-people' refugees.) When launching this campaign, Benetton announced (though not on the billboards) that its intention was 'to call attention to a subject too often ignored by society'.

Three zero-positive individuals sought damages on the basis that this campaign, whatever may have been Benetton's intention (and although the billboards did not identify them), victimized them as members of a group. They said they had suffered an 'assault' on their private lives, reminding them of their status as social outcasts. An association created

---

[14] Roulet, *Le caractère artificiel de la théorie de l'abus de droit en droit international public*, p. 46, n. 30.

to support the victims of AIDS presented itself as an intervening party, acting in the 'collective interests' of afflicted individuals and seeking an order that the billboards be taken down, as well as symbolic monetary damages of one franc.

The complaints were based on Article 1382 of the Civil Code, which is the general foundation of liability in tort, and provides in the broadest terms imaginable (a single sentence of twenty-three words) that those who do wrong are liable for the damages they cause. The plaintiffs rejected Benetton's claim that it was exercising its right to freedom of expression on the grounds of abuse of right.

The Court noted but dismissed Benetton's claim that its campaign intended to evoke sympathy for AIDS victims, stating that the company's explanations were 'unconvincing'. The judges wrote that 'in the current state of knowledge' the AIDS virus is a 'fearful affliction ... likely to generate more or less conscious manifestations of exclusion or rejection, indeed hostility' and that the sight of naked human torsos 'evokes Nazi barbarity or the stamping of meat'. This, the judges found, caused injury to AIDS victims and entitled them to symbolic compensation and an injunction to stop Benetton's campaign.[15]

The Court of Appeals of Paris affirmed the judgment.[16] It added its own reasoning: because the images were not accompanied by any words conveying the intended message, Benetton had used 'degrading symbolism affecting the dignity of individuals implacably afflicted in their body and being, likely to generate or accentuate a phenomenon of rejection'. Even if this form of 'communication' might not be unanimously condemned by the community of victims or by the public at large, this harm could not be excused by Benetton's commitment, however sincere, to the fight against AIDS.

The case attracted considerable but ephemeral attention in the general press, but very little by way of legal analysis. One succinct case note appeared in the wake of the decision of the *Tribunal de grande instance*,[17] doing little more than to state the facts and express the view that the judgment was consistent with the Preamble of the Universal Declaration of Human Rights as well as with French constitutional principles. Its author also observed that the French Penal Code forbids both '*atteintes à*

---

[15] Association Aides federation nationale c. Sté Benneton Group Spa, 1 February 1995, *Recueil Dalloz* 1995.569.

[16] Sté Benneton Group Spa c. Association Aides federation nationale, 27 May 1996, RG 95/12571.

[17] B. Edelman, case note, *Receuil Dalloz* (1995), 569.

la dignité de la personne' and discrimination, while the second chapter of
the Civil Code (in nine sub-articles) imposes 'respect for the human
body' (literally *respect du corps humain*). He also explained that the
Tribunal de grande instance had given Benetton 'a lesson in the deontology of advertising', which he applauded with fervour. As for the Court of
Appeal's confirmation of that judgment, it was reported along with
another note that simply approved both courts as well as the reference
to the Universal Declaration.[18]

Whether advertising is offensive depends on the community where it
takes place. (Billboards in Paris routinely show images that would be
unthinkable on the streets of the United States and severely punishable in
many non-Western countries.) Moreover, there may be differences of
views as to whether advertising is subject to the same rules as 'speech'.
The forms of specific regulation of advertising vary from country to
country, as do the types of sanctions for violations. To the extent that
advertisers enjoy the right of freedom of expression, its limits are also set
by law. In France, such limits are prominently defined in the venerable
Loi sur la Presse du 29 juillet 1881 and its numerous amendments, which
cover far more than the press – extending even to posts in social media.
Did the judges in *Benetton* implicitly believe that such legislation is
unnecessary, since everything can fall under the notion of abusing the
right of 'free' expression?

The first of the case comments referred to above unintentionally
pointed to what was wrong in *Benetton*, when its author applauded the
judges for having given a lesson of advertising deontology to the company. Judges are not nannies. Any such lessons are, in the first instance, to
be the product of deliberations of regulators and the representatives of
the industry and the public – a form of collaboration that establishes
evolving codes for the industry and thus typically set out the rules to live
by. The outcomes thus generated may cause the legislature to step in and
impose corrections. What the particular judges who happened to hear the
Benetton came up with, after hearing the particular arguments of the
particular parties involved in that case, seems based on criteria derived
from nothing but their personal inspiration; no authority is quoted to
justify the weight given to their belief that carriers of the AIDS virus were
likely to experience feelings of rejection upon seeing Benetton's billboards, or that the sight of naked torsos evoked 'Nazi brutality', while
giving none to Benetton's claim that its campaign was intended to

---

[18] T. Hassler, case note, *Receuil Dalloz* (1997), 89.

generate sympathy for victims too often ignored. By reference to what criteria did the Court of Appeal consider it relevant that the billboards had not identified the intended 'message', and irrelevant that parts of the 'community of victims or the public at large' might not be offended, and equally irrelevant that Benetton may have been sincerely engaged in the fight against AIDS?

Above all, why did all the judges ignore the most obvious manifestation of legislative intent, to be found in the first pages of the Civil Code in the nine above-mentioned sub-articles of the chapter entitled *Du respect du corps humain*? All of these, according to the final Article 16-9, are matters of non-derogable public policy. Article 16 as a whole has provided the basis for innumerable decisions related to various forms of violations of the human dignity, including precisely the publications of images of human bodies.[19] Did the judges in *Benetton* implicitly believe that the Civil Code itself is now unnecessary, since they can decide everything in light of their sentiments as to whether a right has been abused?

The *Benetton* case is an unsettling example of how the handy but nebulous notion of abuse of right may be enlisted to justify the outcome of a legal dispute without invoking more meaningful pre-existing criteria. The judges of the two courts that dealt with the matter seemed to be making up justifications for their decision as they went along, thus exercising pure discretion by reference to the most general of precepts. (It is hard to think of anything more elevated than the Preamble of the Universal Declaration of Human Rights.) Benetton did not pursue the matter to the Court of Cassation (which it could have done in France as of right), perhaps because it realised that the controversy was detrimental to its image and preferred to let the matter lie. The plaintiffs had won their symbolic victory and had no reasonable prospect of altering the monetary award at the higher level. Perhaps the best thing that can be said for the case is that it may have triggered a reconsideration of relevant norms by the advertising industry, regulatory and public interest bodies, and ultimately legislators. Surely so important a feature of life in modern society cannot left to be regulated by the feelings and sermonizing of the individual judges who happen to hear a particular case.

---

[19] The Court of Cassation has made it clear that photographs of the bodies of murder victims may not be published if they are motivated by sensationalism; see the notes under Article 16 of any recent editions of the *Dalloz Mega Code Civil*.

The Louisiana Experience

Those who consider the merits or otherwise of importing a general principle based on the notion of abuse of right would do well to focus on a single jurisdiction where this possibility has been invoked and to examine it in some detail. The State of Louisiana seems to serve this purpose well, since it (uniquely among the United States of America) is a civil code jurisdiction, has been directly and significantly influenced by the French Civil Code and jurisprudence, and for the purposes of this book, presents the advantage of posing no issues of translation.

The Supreme Court of Louisiana has professed adherence to 'the theory of abuse of right'.[20] Nevertheless the Civil Code of Louisiana, like that of France, contains no mention of 'abuse of rights'. Courts have instead *inferred* the presence of an intent to forbid the abuse of rights. In the *Hero Lands* case, the Supreme Court found such an intent to be expressed in Articles 667 and 668 of the Code (discussed later), and a concurring judge suggested that the theory 'by analogy and extension . . . can be applied to contractual, delictual, and legal relations other than ownership of property'.

It is worth looking at not only those two Articles, but the next two as well.

> *Art. 667. Limitations on Use of Property.*
>
> Although a proprietor may do with his estate whatever he pleases, still he cannot make any work on it, which may deprive his neighbor of the liberty of enjoying his own, or which may be the cause of any damage to him. However, if the work he makes on his estate deprives his neighbor of enjoyment or causes damage to him, he is answerable for damages only upon a showing that he knew or, in the exercise of reasonable care, should have known that his works would cause damage, that the damage could have been prevented by the exercise of reasonable care, and that he failed to exercise such reasonable care. Nothing in this Article shall preclude the court from the application of the doctrine of *res ipsa loquitur* in an appropriate case. Nonetheless, the proprietor is answerable for damages without regard to his knowledge or his exercise of reasonable care, if the damage is caused by an ultrahazardous activity. An ultrahazardous activity as used in this Article is strictly limited to pile driving or blasting with explosives.

---

[20] This expression is found in *Hero Lands Co. v. Texaco, Inc.,* 310 So.2d 93, 99 (La. 1975). A concurring opinion (at p. 99) declared that 'Louisiana adopts as a general theory or principle of law that in all areas of legal relationships a legal right can be exercised in such a manner as to constitute legal abuse. An abusive use of a legal right may be enjoined or may give rise to damages.'

Art. 668. Inconvenience to Neighbor.

Although one be not at liberty to make any work by which his neighbor's buildings may be damaged, yet every one has the liberty of doing on his own ground whatsoever he pleases, although it should occasion some inconvenience to his neighbor.

Thus he who is not subject to any servitude originating from a particular agreement in that respect, may raise his house as high as he pleases, although by such elevation he should darken the lights of his neighbor's house, because this act occasions only an inconvenience, but not a real damage.

Art. 669. Regulation of Inconvenience.

If the works or materials for any manufactory or other operation, cause an inconvenience to those in the same or in the neighboring houses, by diffusing smoke or nauseous smell, and there be no servitude established by which they are regulated, their sufferance must be determined by the rules of the police, or the customs of the place.

Art. 670. Encroaching Building.

When a landowner constructs in good faith a building that encroaches on an adjacent estate and the owner of that estate does not complain within a reasonable time after he knew or should have known of the encroachment, or in any event complains only after the construction is substantially completed the court may allow the building to remain. The owner of the building acquires a predial servitude [Also written as *praedial*, comparable to an easement at common law.] on the land occupied by the building upon payment of compensation for the value of the servitude taken and for any other damage that the neighbor has suffered.

Significantly, legislation explicitly embracing the notion of abuse of right was considered and rejected in the context of a project for a revision of the Civil Code. The draft included the following provisions:

Art. 661. Abnormal Use of Property.

An act, activity, or work of a property owner that, under the circumstances existing when it is done, exceeds the normal exercise of the right of ownership constitutes an abuse of the right.

An abuse of right of ownership that may cause damage to another or deprive him of the enjoyment of his property subjects the property owner to responsibility.

Art. 662. Unreasonable Use of Estate.

An unreasonable use of an estate that causes damage to property or excessive discomfort to persons of normal sensibilities by the diffusion of smoke, duct, vapor, noise, heat, vibrations, odors, and the like, may be enjoined. Damages may be recovered without regard to defendant's negligence.

Whether the use of an estate is unreasonable is determined in light of the nature of the neigborhood, governmental regulations, local customs, and the attending circumstances.

These two proposed Articles were rejected in the course of the legislative process. Athanassios Yiannopoulos, a prominent scholar of Louisiana law, nevertheless insisted that 'an amorphous and innominate abuse of right doctrine' is to be found in 'scattered provisions of the Civil Code'.[21]

At the same time, Yiannopoulos acknowledged that in the end, 'express reference to "abuse of right" was meticulously avoided'.[22] Moreover, he describes the reality on the ground as follows:

> No reported decision has been found … in which a Louisiana court has held a particular act or activity to be an abuse of ownership solely by reference to the doctrine of abuse of right. Ordinarily, Louisiana courts award damages or issue injunctions under the authority of Articles 667–669 of the Louisiana Civil Code without express reference to the abuse of right doctrine. In such case, however, the imposition of civil responsibility is often justified by the unexpressed realisation that under the established facts the defendant had abused his ownership. It follows that examples of acts and activities that constitute abuse of the right of ownership are found in the rich jurisprudence dealing with the obligations of neighbourhood rather than in decisions applying the doctrine of abuse of right.

And:

> It is now common practice for counsel in Louisiana to add a count of abuse of right in a petition seeking redress in matters of conventional obligations and contracts. In response, courts routinely recite the criteria for abuse of right as if they were articles of faith[23] and typically conclude that, under the circumstances and the evidence adduced at trial, there has

---

[21] A. N. Yiannopoulos, 'Civil Liability for Abuse of Right: Something Old, Something New …', 54 *Louisiana Law Review* (1994), 1173, at 1176.

[22] Yiannopoulos, 'Civil Liability for Abuse of Right', 1176.

[23] These are not found in the Civil Code but have been generated by judicial pronouncements. They are: '(1) the exercise of rights exclusively for the purpose of harming another or with the predominant motive to cause harm; (2) the non-existence of a serious and legitimate interest that is worthy of judicial protection; (3) the use of the right in violation of moral rules, good faith, or elementary fairness; or (4) the exercise of the right for a purpose other than that for which it was granted.' See *210 Baronne St. Ltd. Partnership v. First Nat'l Bank of Commerce*, 543 So.2d 502, 507 (La. App. 4th Cir.), writ denied, 546 So.2d 1219 (1989).

been no abuse of right. *The doctrine of abuse of right is thus largely honored by lip service* rather than as ground for the recovery of injunctive relief. It is rare, indeed, that a Louisiana court has found an abuse of right in the framework of the law of obligations and contracts.[24]

Having given this account, Yiannopoulos insisted that there was none-theless no 'cause for alarm' because

> Louisiana courts have ... reached commendable results in accordance with contractual provisions and by direct application of the governing provisions of the Louisiana Civil Code governing conventional obliga-tions and contracts ... reaching the same results that could also be achieved by application of the abuse of right doctrine.[25]

But why should one have any concern at all that there is 'cause for alarm'? When the legislature makes an effort at targeted and specific definitions of the legal consequences designed to induce behaviour that is consistent with a general, abstract principle that we all agree with, why should we regret the loss of judicial opportunity to elevate their reasoning to the level of more amorphous abstractions? Why insist on the 'unex-pressed realisation' that conduct falls in the category of abuse of rights, and why indeed not content one's self that the courts engage in the 'direct application' of the law?

Yiannopoulos went to lengths to stress that the positive law in Louisiana 'embodies the premises of the abuse of right doctrine'.[26] He was undoubtedly right, but why should it matter? His answer was that 'the general doctrine of abuse of right is needed to explain the foundation underlying those articles and to set the limits beyond which the exercise of the right of ownership engages civil responsibility'.[27] This is unpersuasive. The only explanation 'needed' by citizens, lawyers, and judges for Articles 667–70 of the Louisiana Civil Code is that the legislature felt that controversies regarding matters that fall under their specific rubrics should be resolved as there set forth. The gloss of a lofty abstraction might be of interest as a matter of legal history, but that presupposes a willingness to engage in greater depth than quoting a phrase. As for the second part of the answer – 'to set the limits' – the suggestion seems to be that even where the law-maker has defined limits of specific applicability there

---

[24] Yiannopoulus, 'Civil Liability for Abuse of Right', 1185. Emphasis added.
[25] Yiannopoulus, 'Civil Liability for Abuse of Right'.
[26] Yiannopoulus, 'Civil Liability for Abuse of Right'.
[27] Yiannopoulus, 'Civil Liability for Abuse of Right'.

must be room for judicial authority to decide cases by reference to a higher but more amorphous norm.

Concluding his study in a proselytising vein, Yiannopoulos wrote that the oft-repeated criteria conceived by the Louisiana courts[28] (although 'largely honoured by lip service' and courts 'typically conclude that, under the circumstances and the evidence adduced at the trial, there has been no abuse of rights'),[29] the indeterminateness of the definition of abuse of right, and the 'concerns' that it engenders, should be tolerated because somehow it

> is preferable to a 'can't be done' approach. We should not give up the effort to define the abuse of right even if we were to admit that the debate over the meaning of abuse of right and the desireability of the application of the doctrine is generated by irreconcilable 'views of human nature and social responsibility.' Moreover, we should not be deterred by the knowledge that 'there are broad divergences among civilians and civil law courts concerning the proper scope and limits' of the abuse of rights doctrine.[30]

Yet it must surely be a cause for alarm that elsewhere the author of the comment quoted by Yiannopoulos in this passage about the conflict between 'human nature and social responsibility' had described his review of the law of Louisiana as 'an unsuccessful search for a coherent framework by which to analyse the doctrine of "abuse of right"',[31] while the fuller statement of the second quoted observation about 'broad divergences', written by a professor from the University of Buenos Aires, reads as follows: 'there are broad divergences among civilians and civil law courts concerning its proper scope and limits. There is still a great deal of discussion as to what are really the grounds covered by the doctrine. At its present stage of development, it is difficult to state neat, clear and precise concepts embodying the doctrine.'[32]

---

[28] Yiannopoulos, 'Civil Liability for Abuse of Right', p. 1180: 'These criteria have been constantly and ceremoniously repeated in Louisiana decisions that may have achieved the status of a *jurisprudence constante*: To justify the application of the doctrine "abuse of rights" one of the following must exist: (1) the exercise of rights exclusively for the purpose of harming another or with the predominant motive to cause harm; (2) the non-existence of a serious and legitimate interest that is worthy of judicial protection; (3) the use of the right in violation of moral rules, good faith or elementary fairness; or (4) the exercise of the right for a purpose other than that for which is was granted.'

[29] Yiannopoulus, 'Civil Liability for Abuse of Right', p. 1185.

[30] Yiannopoulus, 'Civil Liability for Abuse of Right', p. 1196.

[31] S. Herman, 'Classical Social Theories and the Doctrine of "Abuse of Rights"', 37 *Louisiana Law Review* (1977), 747.

[32] J. Cueta-Rua, 'Abuse of Rights', 35 *Louisiana Law Review* (1975), 965, at 971. Cueta-Rua also wrote 'in those countries where it has not been formally acknowledged, jurists and

Moreover, when the 1984 revision of the Code 'meticulously avoided' the words *abuse of right*,[33] it was 'widely believed' that Louisiana utility companies had been opposed to them.[34] A professor, W. T. Tête, declared that he objected to the expression because of the following explanatory comment: 'Generally, there is an abuse of the right of ownership when a landowner uses his property contrary to the social and economic purpose for which the law recognizes the right of ownership in immovable property.' This, Tête explained, was unacceptable to him because it echoed Article 1 of the Civil Code of the Russian Soviet Socialist Republic.[35] Yiannopoulos countered that Tête was simply and rather embarrassingly mistaken; the statement 'merely reflected the formulation of the abuse of rights doctrine in Article 281 of the Civil Code of Greece'.[36]

If this is how the concept looked from the perspective of the State of Louisiana, one of the fifty federated units of one of the multitude of nations of the world, there is every reason to be acutely apprehensive of attempts to universalise it.

More recent developments should not encourage proponents of the expansive application of the notion. A striking example emerged in the aftermath of a case decided by the Louisiana Supreme Court dealing with a local wage forfeiture law that provided, in part, 'No person ... shall require any of his employees to sign contracts by which the employees shall forfeit their wages if discharged before the contract is completed ... but in all such cases the employees shall be entitled to the wages actually earned up to the time of their discharge or resignation.'[37]

In the case in question, the plaintiff had earned an award through his employer's supplemental compensation plan, but had not received the entire award before he was fired.[38] When that happened, the employer refused to waive the plan's non-termination requirement. The result was that he was deprived of what the Court referred to as 'delayed

---

judges have construed traditional rules concerning extra-contractual responsibility, limitations of ownership rights, and good faith in the performance of contractual obligations, in such a manner that the doctrine of abuse of rights is said to be one of the underlying principles of the national law'.

[33] Yiannopoulos, 'Civil Liability for Abuse of Right', 1196.

[34] Yiannopoulos, 'Civil Liability for Abuse of Right', 1176, n. 12.

[35] W. T. Tête, 'Tort Roots and the Ramifications of the Obligations Revisions', 32 *Loyola Law Review* (1986), 47, at 71, n. 93.

[36] Yiannopoulos, 'Civil Liability for Abuse of Right', 1176, n. 12.

[37] *La. Rev. Stat. Ann.* § 23:634.

[38] *Morse v. J. Ray McDermott & Co., Inc.*, 344 So.2d 1353 (La. 1977).

compensation, or pay, for performed services' and held that the employer's failure to waive the plan's non-termination requirement constituted abuse of a legal right. But since the detriment to the employee was the forfeiture of 'already earned compensation', the result is better understood as the simple result of applying the just-quoted *lex specialis*.

This observation is powerfully strengthened by considering a 1992 judgment where the United States Court of Appeals for the Fifth Circuit, sitting in New Orleans and applying Louisiana law, reasoned as follows in considering another claim for forfeiture by a terminated employee:[39]

> The abuse of rights doctrine set out in *Morse* has absolutely no application to this case. .... There is no indication in the record that Georgia Gulf's employee stock plan was meant to compensate employees for their services. In fact, the stated purpose of the stock plan was to provide employees with 'additional incentives to achieve the Company's objectives through participation in its success and growth and by encouraging their continued association with the Company'. There is also no evidence that Lloyd's salary and/or employee benefits would have changed had he decided not to take part in the stock plan. Simply put, by refusing to waive the vesting requirement, Georgia Gulf did not forfeit any wages that Lloyd had earned through the performance of his job duties. His stock claim has absolutely no basis in the law and should not have been presented to the jury.

For present purposes, an even more significant statement is found in footnote four of this judgment, which follows the first sentence just quoted and reads as follows:

> In addition to this conclusion, we should also point out that neither the Louisiana Supreme Court, nor the Louisiana courts of appeal, have applied the abuse of rights doctrine since the *Morse* case in 1977. *Furthermore, it is clear that the abuse of rights doctrine is not even a fully established legal concept in Louisiana.* (Citations omitted; emphasis added.)

An equally emphatic assertion to the same effect by the Court of Appeals for the Fifth Circuit in 2004, in a heavily litigated case that refers back to *Lloyd* v. *Georgia Gulf* with approval, is quoted below.[40]

Himpurna: An Unnecessary Claim of Universality

As stated in my foreword, I signed an award in 1999 that contained the words 'the principle of abuse of right is universal' and invoked them as

---

[39] *Lloyd* v. *Georgia Gulf Corp.*, 961 F 2d 1190 (5th Cir. 1992).
[40] See note 47 of this chapter.

a self-sufficient rule of decision. But I have long since repented. A review
of the circumstances of that case may provide an occasion for useful
reflection.

The just-quoted phrase appeared in two substantially identical awards
rendered in a complex case usually referred to simply as *Himpurna
v. Indonesia.*[41] The Respondent in both of those awards was in fact not
the State of Indonesia, but the national electricity utility, PT. Persero
Perusahaan Listruik Negara ('PLN'). The case involved a set of contracts
rather than a treaty. Two questions arise: What did the statement mean?
And was it correct?

First of all, what did the phrase signify? Let us assume that no one
would seriously suggest that as soon as a tribunal has decided which party
it prefers, it is a universal principle that they can simply declare that the
other party has abused a right.

Legal cases are not decided on an instant understanding of an abstract
phrase: the criteria employed when applying the particular concept are
decisive and must be understood to provide a contextually satisfactory
explanation. For example, one expects the reasoning to make clear how
the concept of abuse of right affects (and perhaps determines) the
entitlements of the parties in light of constitutive elements of that concept
which are set out in the decision. A pithy abstraction is of little assistance
alone.

The claimants in *Himpurna* had presented a USD 2.3 billion claim
against Indonesia on account of electricity-generating geothermal
projects that were cancelled before the commencement of any deliv-
eries. The termination arose in doubly extraordinary circumstances:
(1) the financial meltdown in Asia that commenced in July 1997 and
as far as Indonesia was concerned led to a collapse of the national
currency and a 13.5 per cent drop in the GDP the following year,
and (2) a drastic regime change: after three decades in power, the
Suharto government fell in May 1998 as millions of Indonesians
dropped below the poverty line. *Himpurna* was one of several

---

[41] This case is notorious because of the controversial disappearance of an arbitrator on the
eve of a merits hearing in The Hague, in the subsequent proceedings against the State as
guarantor of PLN's debt, as well as an unsuccessful application to the Dutch court to
enjoin the hearing in the Peace Palace. The presiding arbitrator was the same in both,
chosen by agreement of all parties. The Claimants' appointee was also the same. PLN and
the State appointed two different arbitrators. See *Himpurna California Energy Ltd.
v. Republic of Indonesia*, interim award, 26 September 1999; final award,
16 October 1999; extracts in 25 *ICCA Yearbook Commercial Arbitration* (2000), 109, 186.

cases brought by investors whose capital-intensive projects were terminated.

The cases proceeded in two stages: the first dealing with contractual claims against PNL and the second with the Indonesian State's guarantees of PNL's obligations. The Final Awards against PNL in May 1999 were rendered by a majority that included a retired judge of the Indonesian Supreme Court and me.[42] The phrase quoted here to the effect that 'the principle of abuse of right is universal' cites no other legal authority than 'chapter 4' of Bin Cheng's *General Principles*,[43] without any specific quotation or other substantiation.

The discussion of abuse of right came at the end of lengthy award, under the title 'Hypothetical profits on investments not yet made'. The relevant contract contained a provision (Article 8.3) to the effect that 'the Tribunal need not be bound by strict rules of law', and deferred to the arbitrators' judgment as to the 'correct and just enforcement of this agreement'. In other words, there was a contractual warrant to give weight to considerations of fairness irrespective of 'strict rules of law'. The majority of the Tribunal was thus authorized to devise the solution it thought 'correct and just'.

The phrase 'abuse of right' was invoked to explain two arbitrators' decision to limit the recovery of lost profits as follows. Having found a breach of contract, the majority did not wish to allow vast profits that the claimant might have earned from those of its production facilities that had *not yet been built,* and therefore reduced that part of the claims by some 90 per cent.[44] PNL had contracted to purchase and pay for the entirety of the Claimants' output in USD, whereas its only possible onward sales were exclusively on the national market, priced in rupiah, the Indonesian currency that had lost 80 per cent of its USD value as a result of the Asian financial crisis. The Claimants were seeking the aforementioned USD 2.3 billion return on a USD 315 million investment – namely earnings from hypothetical sales to PNL, a public utility *not* created for profit that could have done

---

[42] The Final Awards are published in *Measley's International Arbitration Report*, vol. 14, 12/99, at A-1.

[43] A citation to a study conducted by Professor Karl-Heinz Böckstiegel concerned an unrelated issue.

[44] *Himpurna California Energy Ltd.* v. *Republic of Indonesia*, interim award, 26 September 1999; final award, 16 October 1999; extracts in 25 *ICCA Yearbook Commercial Arbitration* (2000), 109. See Final Awards published in *Measley's International Arbitration Report*, vol. 14, 12/99, at A-1, at para. 587.

nothing with the electricity except to sell it on the national market at a ruinous discount.

At the time the dispute arose, the Indonesian public institutions were in evident disarray given the fall of a discredited government that had for so long dominated all public institutions. From all reports, the wholesale replacement of officials took place in a context of understandable confusion and disorganisation, not least when it came to dealing with a large international arbitration brought by sophisticated investors represented by international lawyers of the first rank.

The two arbitrators forming the majority started off by stating that they would apply

> the doctrine of abuse of right as an element of overriding substantive law proper to the international arbitral process. This is not an elaborate body of law. It has been applied notably when arbitral tribunals have upheld the principle of the autonomy of the arbitration clause or refused to accept that a State invokes its internal law as an impediment to its consent to arbitration.[45]

The pronoun 'it' at the beginning of the third sentence refers to 'overriding substantive law proper to the international arbitral process' and not to 'the doctrine of abuse of right'; this is easily verified by noting that neither of the examples given nor the footnote references to *Benteler*, Schwebel, and Böckstiegel at the end of the quoted passage have anything to do with abuse of right. It cannot be inferred from the recognition of the existence of overriding norms that 'abuse of right' is recognised by the cited authorities as being one of them; that would be non sequitur.

The award then goes on to make the already quoted affirmation: 'the principle of abuse of right is universal'. The only cited authority is Cheng's chapter 4; and 'this' rule is described as having an obverse formulation: 'good faith in the exercise of rights'. For this I can only express regret; as we have seen, Cheng's chapter 4 clearly distinguished between the *principle* of good faith and the 'theory' of abuse of right, and we know from his foreword to Roulet's book that Cheng explicitly did not make any claim to resolve the debatable status of that theory.

The *Himpurna* majority's invocation of abuse of right was met with both doubt and criticism, which emerged in the first instance from the dissenting opinion of the Australian co-arbitrator, who wrote that he was:

---

[45] *Himpurna California Energy Ltd.* v. *Republic of Indonesia*, para. 528.

particularly troubled by the novel proposition that the Claimant's reliance upon its contractual rights . . . amounts to an abuse of rights thus leading to and permitting a substantial reduction of what might otherwise be rewarded.

My concern is that such a questionable proposition and its manner of application in this Award prejudices notions of legal security and basic principles of private law.

I note that every doubt in respect of *lucrum cessans* have been determined favorably for the Respondent.

The imposition of a concept described as 'abuse of right' in the absence of findings of malicious intent or lack of good faith on the part of the Claimant to further reduce the entitlement to damages is in my opinion an inappropriate and unwarranted penalizing of the Claimant.

In addition to the fact that there was a contractual acknowledgment of the arbitral tribunal's authority to give weight to considerations of fairness, the following additional elements were present in *Himpurna* and merit emphasis: (1) the award invoked abuse of rights prospectively, to prevent an excessive award of damages on account of the loss of profits that would have been earned from investments not yet made, with no mention, let alone consideration, of abuse of right in the context of jurisdiction or as a means to deprive a claimant of its access to arbitration; and (2) *Himpurna* was in line with three ICSID arbitrations cited as examples of reducing amounts awarded for lost profits that were not concerned with the governmental *takeover* of a profitable venture but *interference* with it.[46]

For some time after the *Himpurna* decision, I maintained my view of the notion of abuse of right as a general principle, until I took the time one summer to read the actual materials to which Cheng's chapter 4 refers – and concluded that it was untenable. (It is essential to overcome the confusion that seems to follow from the fact that the word 'abuse' is everywhere, and to see that (1) *abusive conduct* can generate legal consequences without involving the abuse of *a right*, (2) *abuse of process* is misuse *of an institution* even in the absence of mischievous intent, and (3) even in those legal systems where *abuse of right proper* is held to be a principle, it is limited to rare and curious circumstances.) It would surprise me that anyone would consider the *Himpurna* award a significant precedent with respect to abuse of rights, given that the

---

[46] *Southern Pacific Properties* v. *Egypt*, ICSID Case No. ARB/84/3, award, 20 May 1992; *Societe Ouest Africaine des Betons Industriels* v. *Senegal*, ICSID Case No. ARB/82/1, award, 25 February 1988; and *Asian Agricultural Products Ltd* v. *Sri Lanka*, ICSID Case No. ARB/87/3, award, 8 April 2013.

phrase in question is a simple assertion with no identification of the elements of the supposed principle, or analysis of how they might have been satisfied in the particular situation. At any rate, I am not aware of it having attracted a jurisprudential following.[47]

Looking back, I find no difficulty in seeing the outcome in *Himpurna* as being consistent with Lauterpacht's statement to the effect that any legal right 'may, in some circumstances, be refused recognition on the ground that it has been abused' that seems uncontroversial, although hardly a rule of decision since it fails to identify 'the circumstances' in question.[48] The heart of the matter is how, in a particular case, one may identify and articulate the legal basis for giving effect to this limitative effect apart from employing the word 'abuse'. The vast corpus of the common law has never embraced the term 'abuse of law', and even in those civil law countries where it is applied, this happens only in cases too unusual to provide meaningful general precedents, and even then with all sorts of qualifications and variations as to the elements required to deny a right. Repeating a phrase to support a desired outcome is not the same thing as applying – let alone *establishing* – a legal principle.

When *Himpurna* was decided, the UNIDROIT *Principles of International Commercial Contracts* had not yet seen the light of day. As seen in Chapter 1, they do not mention 'abuse of rights'. Some might nonetheless be tempted first to deem the general rule of good faith[49] to encompass abuse of rights and then (notwithstanding the cacophony of definitions) to rely on the Official Comment to Article 1.7, where the expression 'abuse of right' is actually employed, to explain how it might be characterised as something falling under the Article: 'a party's malicious behavior which occurs for instance when a party exercises a right merely to damage the other party or for a purpose other than the one for

---

[47] In the course of heavily-litigated enforcement actions in the United States, the respondent in *Karaha Bodas Co. v. Perusahaam Pertambangan Minyak Dan Gas Bumi Negara et al.*, 364 F 3d 274, n. 103 (5th Cir. 2004), sought to invoke the doctrine of abuse of rights as an obstacle to enforcement under the public policy exception of the New York Convention on the Recognition and Enforcement of Foreign Arbitral Awards. The federal Fifth Circuit Court of Appeals (based in Louisiana) rejected the argument, stating flatly that '[t]he abuse of rights doctrine is not established in American law', followed by note 103 to this effect: 'The abuse of rights doctrine is not even fully established in Louisiana, the American jurisdiction that has invoked it,' citing *Lloyd v. Georgia Gulf Corp.*, 961 F 2d 1190, 1193, n. 4 (5th Cir. 1992).

[48] See Chapter 6, text following note 6.

[49] The relevant text is Article 1.7: 'Each party must act in accordance with good faith and fair dealing in international trade.'

which it had been granted, or when the exercise of the right is disproportionate to the originally intended result.'

The notion of disproportionality 'to the originally intended result' is
interesting and seems apposite to the circumstances in *Himpurna*. But
there is no evidence of its acceptance as part of the applicable Indonesian
law. In the end, the safest rationale for the outcome was the contractual
stipulation that 'the Tribunal need not be bound by strict rules of law' and
the arbitrators were mandated to exercise their judgment as to the
'correct and just enforcement of this agreement'. In other circumstances,
to restate a *Leitmotif* of this book, the applicable *lex specialis* might grant
similar explicit discretion to the decision-maker. But for a court or
tribunal intuitively to invent the content of the abstraction *abuse of
right* is to step onto a path of arbitrariness.[50]

---

[50] I thus find myself in agreement with one of the early comments on the case (see I. Petrova,
"'Stepping on the Shoulders of a Drowning Man" – The Doctrine of Abuse of Right as
a Tool for Reducing Damages for Lost Profits: Troubling Lessons from the Patuha and
Himpurna Arbitrations', 35 *Georgetown Journal of International Law* (2004), 455), concluding thus at pages 481–2: 'Although the general idea that rights should not be abused is
not controversial, there is great difficulty in fashioning a set of rules for determining when
an abuse has occurred that will yield consistent results when applied to different factual
situations. Although there is a good argument to be made that the outcome in the *Patuha*
and *Himpurna* arbitration was fair, the reduction in the amount of damages awarded to
the project companies demonstrated the danger inherent in the abuse of right reasoning.
A broad formulation of the doctrine allows for a great deal of discretion that may lead to
analytically strained results and undermine notions of legal certainty.'

The infinite variety of ephemeral arbitral tribunals may well use abuse of right as a high-sounding phrase to justify their intuitions, but it takes more than that to establish a general principle of international law under the Statute of the International Court of Justice. The Court itself has never decided a case on the basis of abuse of right. In one of its judgments in 2018, its prudence with respect to such abstract notions was illustrated by refusal to accept 'legitimate expectations' as a general principle.

5

The Challenge of Establishing Universal Principles

We now move from the national to the international. This chapter considers what would be required for the notion of abuse of right to become a principle of international law, with particular reference to Article 38(1) of the Statute of the International Court of Justice ('ICJ'). Chapter 6 reviews the objectives and efforts of two eminent scholars who launched the project in the 1920s. Chapter 7 describes the intellectual and jurisprudential mid-century pushback, and the realistic retreat of a new generation of defenders who implicitly abandoned the quest for international recognition of the notion of abuse of right as a free-standing principle of international law. The concluding Chapter 8 seeks to fix our position two decades into the twenty-first century.

Article 38(1) of the ICJ Statute

What entitles a supposed principle to be part of international law? Put in other terms, who has the authority to *proclaim* international law? In the absence of a planetary parliament, it is a vexed question. 'Professors' is a response likely to elicit mirth. 'Heads of government' would perhaps cause lamentation. The best we can do is to examine the decisions of international courts and tribunals, to identify the rules they apply (whether expressly or implicitly), and to appraise the reception given to those rules as they are set adrift on the sea of international criticism.

At first glance, this notion of *the best we can do* is not particularly promising, given the profusion of 'international courts and tribunals' and the fact that in the course of generations, they have given varied answers to the question that concerns us here. But the International Court of Justice, as the 'principal judicial organ of the United Nations', has made the most influential attempt to define the 'sources' of international law (in fact perpetuating the efforts of the League of Nations and its creation: the Permanent Court of International Justice, a short-lived and less-inclusive precursor of the ICJ). The result now appears as Article 38(1) of the Statute of the ICJ. International lawyers know it more or less by heart. It defines four sources of international law – that is, the collective repository of rules of decision by which disputes under international law should be resolved. These four categories are listing in descending order of importance as follows:

a. international conventions, whether general or particular, establishing rules expressly recognised by the contesting states;
b. international custom, as evidence of a general practice accepted as law;
c. the general principles of law recognised by civilised nations; and
d. subject to the provisions of Article 59, judicial decisions and the teachings of the most highly qualified publicists of the various nations, as subsidiary means for the determination of rules of law.

This book is primarily concerned with the acceptance or otherwise of abuse of right as a 'general principle' under (c). It is useful to begin by considering why the three other 'sources of international law' are of lesser interest.

Paragraph (a)

It is trite but essential to remember that treaties are predominant in international law. States are fiercely jealous of their sovereignty. Like all of us, they prefer rules of their own making, or at least legitimised by their explicit consent. Unlike the rest of us, they are not subject to the edicts of a plenipotentiary legislature that may impose rules. Although states have with some frequency subjected themselves to the adjudicatory authority of courts and tribunals that apply international law, the establishment of the rules to be applied is an exceedingly sensitive matter. Decisions that apply the terms of treaties are on the safest ground. It is unrealistic to expect that any treaty would state in general terms that its signatories agree that 'abuse of right' will be a delict under international law – for the reason that they would not be sure what they were signing up to.

Of course, this does not mean that anyone approves of the abuse of rights. To the contrary, under the circumstances of a particular treaty, it may be highly desirable to prohibit abuse of the rights created under it, and therefore, given the unpredictable ways in which those particular rights might otherwise be invoked, to produce specific, contextually appropriate safeguards. The same need may also result in the explicit grant of adjudicatory discretion to reject claims of right found to be contextually abusive. The best-known example is Article 300 of the 1982 United Nations Convention on the Law of the Sea, which reads as follows: 'States Parties shall fulfil in good faith the obligations assumed under this Convention and shall exercise the rights, jurisdiction and freedoms recognized in this Convention in a manner which would not constitute an abuse of right.'

It is not hard to infer why this unusual grant of discretion appeared in a treaty creating oceanic law. Historically, sovereignty has been, above all, territorial. Even counting the small fringes of so-called territorial sea that surround coastal states, two-thirds of our planet is not territorial in this venerable sense. Although the oceans become ever more domesticated – perhaps too often unilaterally – the need for maritime international cooperation is evident, and there is less resistance to agreement to comprehensive rules, including the grant of discretion to fill possible gaps.

Hence Article 300. Its drafting history should give us pause, and so should the two instances in the course of the ensuing decades when it has been invoked. The Article had its origin in this proposal by Mexico:

> The States Parties to the present Convention undertake . . . to exercise the rights and jurisdictions recognized in the present Convention in such a way that they do not unnecessarily or arbitrarily harm the rights of other States or the interests of the international community as a whole; [and] to discharge in good faith the obligations entered into in conformity with the present Convention.[1]

In the course of the ensuing discussion, Chile stated that it 'supported the Mexican delegation's proposal . . . that reference should be made to two principles of the highest importance: good faith and non-abuse of rights'.[2] One notes that the expression 'non-abuse of rights' did not appear in the Mexican draft. Uruguay responded that 'the substantive part of the convention should contain a precise definition of the principle

---

[1] Official Records of the Third United Nations Conference on the Law of the Sea, vol. IX, Seventh Session, A.CONF. 62/L.25, 5 May 1978, p. 182.

[2] Official Records of the Third United Nations Conference on the Law of the Sea, vol. IX, Seventh Session, 98th Plenary Meeting, A.CONF. 62/SR. 98, 15 May 1978, p. 44.

of non-abuse of rights'.[3] Unsurprisingly, no such definition emerged. Pakistan, for its part, expressed the view that 'the general provision on abuse of rights should be included in the preamble, since it was not substantive but simply declaratory'.[4] Swaziland, on the other hand, stated somewhat curiously, and perhaps contradictorily, that '[t]he general provision concerning abuse of rights was hardly necessary, for it would be difficult to define the notion of "abuse"'.[5]

A Report on the informal plenary discussion summarised the various delegations' views as follows:

> While the first paragraph appeared to be acceptable to most delegations, a few considered it unnecessary as it embodied a general principle of international law incorporated in Article 2 of the Charter of the United Nations.
>
> The second paragraph of this proposal, however, met with some criticism as it was not in accord with some legal systems, certain concepts were not sufficiently founded, and there was a problem of interpretation in some languages. Accordingly, it was decided that consultations should be carried out by interested delegations to attempt to arrive at a compromise text which has meaning and content in all languages and for all legal systems. A revised proposal was subsequently presented.[6]

The text ultimately adopted was proposed as a compromise in March 1980 in a negotiating subgroup, and thereafter accepted by consensus in August 1980 'on the understanding that the article on good faith and abuse of rights was *to be interpreted as meaning that the abuse of rights was in relation to those of other States*'.[7] The words here reproduced in italics introduce a new complexity without resolving it: situating abuse of rights as something to consider in some unspecified way in relation to *overlapping and possibly competing rights*.

The concern was apparently *infringement* more than abuse. The original Mexican proposal, drafted without the words *abuse of rights*, was to forbid states from 'unnecessarily or arbitrarily harming the rights of

---

[3] Official Records of the Third United Nations Conference on the Law of the Sea, vol. IX, Seventh Session, 98th Plenary Meeting, A.CONF. 62/SR. 98, 15 May 1978, p. 46.

[4] Official Records of the Third United Nations Conference on the Law of the Sea, vol. IX, Seventh Session, 106th Plenary Meeting, A/CONF.62.SR.106, 19 May 1978, p. 84.

[5] Official Records of the Third United Nations Conference on the Law of the Sea, vol. IX, Seventh Session, 106th Plenary Meeting, A/CONF.62.SR.106, 19 May 1978, p. 86.

[6] Official Records of the Third United Nations Conference on the Law of the Sea, vol. XIII, Ninth Session, Reports of the President on the work of the informal plenary meeting of the Conference on general provisions, A/CONF.62/L.53, 29 March and 1 April 1980, p. 87.

[7] Official Records of the Third United Nations Conference on the Law of the Sea, vol. XIV, Resumed Ninth Session, Report of the President on the work of the informal plenary meeting of the Conference on general provisions, A/CONF.62/L.58, 22 August 1980, pp. 128–9.

other States or the interests of the international community as a whole'. Given the degree of general assent to the Mexican proposal, it is difficult to imagine that the consensus that emerged was concerned with anything more than the possibility of collision of rights, or between a right and overriding policies of the international community (all in the context of the specific grant of adjudicatory discretion under the law of the sea). Who could imagine that states would accept, à la Josserand, the curtailment of *non-overlapping* rights whenever judges or arbitrators might find their exercise excessive or otherwise unfair?

Still, neither Article 300 nor the quoted 'understanding' gives us specific instructions as to how to reconcile competing rights. As we shall see in Chapter 8, the reductionist version of the notion of abuse of rights that emerged from Alexandre Kiss's celebrated thesis in 1952 focused squarely on use of the concept as an indispensable remedy for the incompatibility of overlapping plenary sovereignties with world order – a matter unique to public international law and one that needs to be resolved by treaty.

So much for the drafting history. The two isolated instances where states have invoked this Article 300 were dealt with by two separate, five-member Tribunals empanelled under the 1982 Convention, perhaps most prominently in *The Philippines* v. *People's Republic of China*. Although China ultimately did not participate in the proceedings, its stance had been set out in a 'Position Paper' that criticised the claim as 'an abuse of the compulsory dispute settlement procedure'. The Tribunal answered that 'the mere act of unilaterally initiating as arbitration under [the Convention] cannot constitute an abuse of rights'[8], quoting the near-identical language used in *Barbados* v. *Trinidad*.[9]

This is, of course, right. If every claim that fails for lack of jurisdiction is to be deemed an abuse of right – as all respondents would soon learn to allege – then every denial of adjudicatory authority would indicate abusiveness. Such provocation of the rejected claimant – hardly conducive to harmonious inter-state relations – is entirely unnecessary, since all that needs to be said is that there is no jurisdiction.

Invoking the spectre of vexatious or frivolous litigation adds nothing to this debate. In order to decide that a claim is vexatious, the adjudicatory body must have jurisdiction. And if it does, it may certainly hold that a claim is frivolous (because it alleges no facts

---

[8] *The Republic of the Philippines* v. *The People's Republic of China*, PCA Case No. 2013–19, award on jurisdiction and admissibility, 29 October 2015, para. 126.

[9] *Barbados* v. *Trinidad and Tobago*, PCA Case No. 2004–02, award, 11 April 2006, para. 205.

that, even if found to be true, state a legal cause of action; or is devoid of any evidentiary foundation) or vexatious (having no purpose save harassment). This is frequently referred to as abuse of process, which should not be confused with abuse of right. Abuse of process is the misuse of an institution; no one has the 'right' to misuse the legal process, and those who seek to do so are properly stopped in accordance with established rules.[10]

The overarching point is that delegation of discretionary authority by treaty – whether couched in the language of equity, abuse of right, or any other indeterminate abstraction – is a matter of *lex specialis* and cannot seriously be put forward as the acknowledgement by treaty of a general, indeterminate prohibition of abuse of right.

Paragraph (b)

The important word here is not *custom*, but the qualifying adjective: *international* custom. Whatever the particularities and inconsistencies of local habits and rules, perhaps we can identify norm-inspiring conduct in the specific context of international relations.[11]

Thus, if we throw up our hands in frustration at the incoherence of national versions of the idea of abuse of right, and give up the quest for a universal general principle, perhaps something can be saved for the international system as such if conduct in that domain might coalesce into a special and useful set of rules. The somewhat elusive distinction might be described as one between general principles generated by international relations and principles generalised from national laws as a source of international law.

---

[10] The caselaw of the ICJ is replete with instances where the principle of abuse of procedure has been invoked. The Court, however, has never found the conditions for an application of the principle to be fulfilled. See A. Zimmermann et al. (eds.), *The Statute of the International Court of Justice: A Commentary*, 2nd ed. (Oxford University Press, 2012), p. 902, n. 20.

[11] Cherif Bassiouni spoke of 'general principles' as 'the underlying or posited principles or postulates of national legal system or of international law', in C. Bassiouni, 'A Functional Approach to "General Principles of International Law"', 11 *Michigan Journal of International Law* (1990), 768. Since Article 38(1)(c) does not refer to 'international law', and since subparagraph (a) refers to explicit law rather than 'underlying or posited principles or postulates' and subparagraph (d) commences with the admonition that even a decision of the ICJ 'has no binding force except between the parties and in respect of that particular case', it seems that subparagraph (b) is the best place for invoking this 'source of international law'.

This is precisely what Helmut Philipp Aust seems to propose in his monograph *Complicity and the Law of State Responsibility*.[12] Abuse of right plays a key role in the foundational chapter, entitled 'Complicity and the Rule of Law'. Aust first sets out what he refers to as 'the principle of abuse of right' and then proceeds to apply it to the problem of complicity. He begins by putting aside the notion of abuse of right *as a general principle* in the sense of Article 38(1)(c), which requires that a proposition be distilled from an observed concordance of national laws. His reason for doing so is that 'some posit that there is no such principle in international law' and 'are sceptical with respect to its scope of application and with respect to its ability to provide normative guidance', adding that 'the debate on the existence of abuse of right as a legal principle in domestic legal orders has proved inconclusive so far'.[13] He is therefore led to search for evidence that abuse of right merits elevation to *an autonomous principle of international law*,[14] and suggests that there is.

We shall see in Chapter 8 that this is an audacious and unwarranted conclusion. If anything, this claim is weaker than the attempt to demonstrate abuse of right as a unifying ('general') principle of national laws, which has been the ambition of most writers who urge acceptance of the notion as a source of international law. For now, some generalities will suffice.

One must be extremely cautious in discerning implicit principles in the actions of states, for *custom* in the sense of Article 38(1)(b) is not reflected in any behaviour of states ('practice'), but a particular species of behaviour: the kind that demonstrates attachment to a constant principle of law rather than the transactional realities of a particular bargain. If accommodations are compelled by force, there is no warrant to see them as recognition of a legal duty. Lawyers express this idea by defining the norm-generating conduct as a product of *opinio juris*, namely

---

[12] H. P. Aust, *Complicity and the Law of State Responsibility* (Cambridge University Press, 2011).

[13] Aust, *Complicity and the Law of State Responsibility*, p. 72. Although he writes at page 71 that '[a]buse of rights is frequently considered to qualify as a general principle of law under Article 38(1)(c)', he makes the frequent mistake of prominently citing Bin Cheng in support of this assertion (Aust, *Complicity and the Law of State Responsibility*, n. 107). The fact is that Cheng referred to it as a *theory* and expressed his admiration (without taking a position) for Roulet's rejection of attempts to elevate it into an international principle; see the second part of Chapter 2.

[14] Aust, *Complicity and the Law of State Responsibility*, p. 72: 'it is this category in which we are interested here'.

a discernible acknowledgement that a course of conduct is chosen because it is accepted as required under law.

The impulse to derive an autonomous international principle is quite understandable. If national systems have not produced a tolerable consensus as to the articulation or operation of a rule preventing the abuse of rights (indeed vanishingly few national systems seem even to have developed *internal* consistency), the quest to elevate the notion to a general principle seems doomed from the start. It is natural to search, as Aust does, for an alternative solution that might somehow give rise to a sui generis principle of international law.

But again, states are protective of their sovereignty, and this jealousy leads to an unwillingness to cede authority to make and apply laws. This explains why treaties are given pride of place as a source of international law; the obligations they establish are not imposed but agreed. The United Nations does not legislate any more than its 'principal judicial organ', the International Court of Justice. It is not difficult to understand that elementary precaution in the interest of its institutional stature – if not survival – commands the ICJ to be slow to derive specific rules of decision from general abstractions. As we shall see, the case for elevation of abuse of right into a principle of international law is weak.

Paragraph (d)

'Judicial decisions' and 'the teachings of the most highly qualified publicists of the various nations' are poor cousins – 'subsidiary' sources that hardly ever figure in the pronouncements of international courts and tribunals except by way of confirming (as opposed to declaring) propositions of law. This is especially true of 'teachings', given the difficulty of identifying 'publicists' worthy of such consideration and in the virtual impossibility in the modern, heterogeneous world of deciding who deserves recognition as 'the most highly qualified'. In any event, with reference to abuse of right in particular, Chapter 6 of this book should largely suffice to dispel any notion that scholarly commentary reflects consensus.

What we have seen so far in this chapter explains why the best (or rather least forlorn) chance to give international status to abuse of right as a principle must be found under Article 38(1)(c), to which we now return.

A Hard Look at Paragraph (c)

The fundamental and immediately apparent understanding of this paragraph is that there is no place for principles of law found *randomly* under *some* national laws; one may invoke only those norms that form part of the principles of law recognised everywhere under national law. The pedigree of such principles needs to be established by something far more serious than the familiarity of stray expressions; abstract propositions do not easily generate useful *rules of decision*.

As Alain Pellet puts it in the 116-page essay devoted to Article 38 in the compendious *Oxford Commentary* on the ICJ Statute:

> The Court itself has referred to Art. 38, para. 1(c) with an extreme parsimony. If the present author is not mistaken, this provision has been expressly mentioned only four times in the entire case law of the Court since 1922 and each time it has been ruled out for one reason or another.[15]

Pellet goes on to write that 'the principles of Art. 38, para(1)(c) ... provide general guidelines which then have to be applied by the Court in the particular case'.[16] Guidelines are not legal rules of decision. The authority to apply them 'in the particular case' should not be a license for arbitrariness.

What we may refer to (in shorthand) as the 'generalisation' of legal principles, generated by a broadly representative cohort of national laws, occurs when they are relied upon to resolve issues faced by courts and tribunals charged with applying international law. If they reflect a consensus in comparative law (or at least an absence of explicit divergence), the application of such national law principles may be uncontroversial. Other principles applied as a matter of national laws may be debatable because they are controversial even as such and therefore also as a matter of comparative law. Yet others may be inconceivable because they simply cannot be assimilated into the framework of international law.

Some general principles that have been well established in national law are easily absorbed into the contexts in which international law applies. For example, when calculating the economic consequences of a breach, be it non-performance of a commercial contract or the wrongful expropriation of a foreigner's property, the principle that victims do not

---

[15] Zimmermann, *The Statute of the International Court of Justice: A Commentary*, p. 833.
[16] Zimmermann, *The Statute of the International Court of Justice: A Commentary*, p. 837.

recover losses they could have mitigated is an equally logical factor in assessing the damages. Similarly, the ILC's *Commentary* on its Articles on State Responsibility identifies a number of criteria for the determination of compensation (under Article 36) that would resonate even with lawyers wholly unacquainted with international law.[17]

There is also broad acceptance that written undertakings are understood to be obligatory with respect to not only what is explicitly stated in the text, but also compliance with the reasonable necessities of performance. The Napoleonic Code's command, in Article 1135 of the Civil Code, that contracts require not only compliance with the text, but also with what is required 'by equity, usage, or law' – still a central feature of French law – has been copied word for word in many countries, perhaps as often in Spanish translation as in French. Modern English lawyers seem to have overcome the reflex to object that their law does not require the good faith performance of contracts, because as they become familiar with 'continental' jurisprudence they can see that it is consonant with the common law's case-by-case determination of implied terms.

Rules of interpretation of legal documents, such as the presumption against redundancy, make such good sense that they too readily migrate – although with awareness that one cannot approach in identical ways the interpretation of a contracts between two parties, the preparation of laws by a parliament comprised of fellow citizens of the same homogenous nations, and a treaty negotiated by delegations from a great number of states having different institutional structures and obedience to conflicting ideologies.

On the other hand, the notion of abuse of right is not easily assimilated into international law[18] for a very simple and fundamental reason having to do with the origin of 'rights'. The rights of the nationals of a country are those bestowed upon them by their sovereign, and it is within the powers of the nation's courts, as emanations of that sovereignty, to restrict the enjoyment of those rights when they say that they have been abused (although as seen prudent legal scholars protest that the definition of rights *include their limitations* and should therefore be a matter for legislative bodies). *The international community is not sovereign.* International law has traditionally been created by its subjects,

---

[17] J. Crawford, *The International Law Commission's Articles on State Responsibility: Introduction, Text and Commentary* (Cambridge University Press, 2002), pp. 218–30.

[18] The index in Chestor Brown's valuable monograph, *A Common Law of International Adjudication* (Oxford University Press, 2007), contains half a dozen entries under the heading 'abuse of process', but none at all under 'abuse of right'.

staunchly protective of their sovereignty. Their rights are generated by self-declaration, and thereafter limited only by their consent. International courts and tribunals purport to limit those rights at the peril of being repudiated, and indeed eroding the authority of international law as a whole. One should not forget how the Permanent Court of International Justice put it in *The Lotus:* 'The rules of law binding upon States ... emanate from their own free will ... Restrictions upon the independence of States cannot therefore be presumed.'[19] There are moments when various actors on the international scene may wish this was not so. Perhaps one day the *Lotus* judgment will be definitively discarded. But, for now, we ignore it at our peril.

---

[19] *The Case of the S.S. Lotus (France* v. *Turkey)*, judgment, 7 September 1927, *P.C.I.J.* Ser. A, No. 10, p. 18.

The attempt to make abuse of right a part of international law was championed by Politis and Lauterpacht in the wake of the horrors of World War I. Their motivation was essentially idealistic, radical, and subversive; they wanted the concept to be used as a tool to overcome the stubborn refusal of states to yield sovereignty.

6

The Politis/Lauterpacht Quest to Elevate the Concept

We have seen that attempts to give meaningful effect to the concept of abuse of right as a tool of decision have led to considerable hesitations, confusion, and controversy within individual national legal systems. It is thus hardly surprising that efforts to derive a consistent and coherent general principle have not produced anything beyond banal and circular generalities, such as the observation that it is abusive to claim more than one's right. One might well replace the word 'abusive' with 'impermissible' to perceive what the French in everyday usage call a *lapalissade*.[1]

This hardly seems a promising foundation for the emergence of a general principle of international law with claims to universality. Yet, in the literature of international law, the concept has paradoxically received a warmer welcome than one would predict in light of its unsettled status under national laws. Such is the likely consequence of an environment where there is more theory than statute, infinitely more scholarly writing than decided cases. In 1958, the uneasy endeavour to elevate abuse of right into the international realm was the focus of Roulet's book-length study, *Le caractère artificiel de la théorie de l'abus de droit en droit international public.*[2]

---

[1] It was reported, so the story goes, that a nobleman named Jacques de la Palice was alive two days before his death. The eponymous expression may have been the result of a misunderstanding; his epitaph affirmed that if he had not died, *il ferait toujours envie* (he would still be envied) that was turned mockingly into *il serait toujours en vie* (he would still be alive).

[2] In a favourable review, Jean Fourré observed that the fact that the very title reveals the author's essential conclusion should not be taken as an a priori presumption (*'un parti pris initial'*); the title is 'the consequence of solidly based study', 12–1 *Revue international de droit comparé* (1960), 289. Fourré, a graduate of the French *Ecole nationale d'administration*, which produces the elite of the French civil service, was to become a member of the *Conseil d'Etat* (the highest court for administrative law). He wrote that Roulet's study had

Precisely focused on attempts to assimilate the notion of abuse of right into international law, Roulet's monograph concluded that: 'If a certain enthusiasm might possibly have been justified during the first years of the League of Nations, the wariness of international tribunals should, however, with our present distance, make us prudent.' It is instructive to consider this record of 'enthusiasm'.

The starting point for the quest to assimilate the notion of abuse of right into international law is widely recognised, namely the famous Politis Lectures, published in 1925 under the title *Le problème des limitations de la souveraineté et la théorie de l'abus de droit dans les rapports internationaux*.[3] They became an enduring lodestar for the invocation of abuse of right with the goal of neutralising what Politis perceived as the excesses of state sovereignty.

Nicolas Politis had studied in France and held law professorships at the Universities of Aix-en-Provence and Paris. He became Greece's Foreign Minister in 1916 as a member of the Venizélos government, and represented Greece in the Paris Peace Conference in 1919. Profoundly marked not only by the obscene carnage of World War I, but also by the devastating consequences of the Greco-Turkish war (1919–20), Politis was instrumental in the creation of the Hague Academy of International Law.[4]

Those who have held the published version of the Politis Lectures in their hands know that the cover displays a title along with a subtitle in much smaller letters. It is worth reproducing it here (as a photocopy of the front cover):

to be robust because it contradicted many theorists – while 'Roulet finds his best allies in the judiciary and his most solid arguments are factual'.

[3] N. Politis, *Le problème des limitations de la souveraineté et la théorie de l'abus de droit dans les rapports internationaux*, vol. I (RCADI, 1925).

[4] In due course, he presided the prestigious Institut de droit international (1937–42).

LE PROBLÈME

DES

LIMITATIONS DE LA SOUVERAINETÉ

ET

LA THÉORIE DE L'ABUS DES DROITS
DANS LES RAPPORTS INTERNATIONAUX

PAR

N. POLITIS

In translation:

THE PROBLEM
OF THE
LIMITATIONS OF SOVEREIGNTY
AND
THE THEORY OF *ABUSE OF RIGHTS*
IN INTERNATIONAL RELATIONS
BY
N. POLITIS

Make no mistake: Politis was not seeking to establish the existence of a legal proposition, but to promote the political objective of neutralising the excesses of state sovereignty. He suggested that 'the theory' of *abus de droit* might be used as a means to that end. Lest there be any doubt, these were his radical words on pages 18–19: *La souveraineté doit être réservé au droit et, pour plus tard, à la communauté internationale. Elle ne peut plus appartenir aux Etats.* ('Sovereignty should be reserved for the law and, in due course, for the international community. It can no longer belong to States.')

Looking back three decades later, in the aftermath of another world war, Georg Schwarzenberger addressed the Grotius Society in London on the topic 'Uses and Abuses of the "Abuse of Rights" in International Law'.[5] His first words were to refer to Politis's 'famous course of lectures'. This was Schwarzenberger's second sentence: 'It did not take long before

---

[5] G. Schwarzenberger, 'Uses and Abuses of the "Abuse of Rights" in International Law', 42 *Transactions of the Grotius Society* (1956), 147–79.

what Politis had modestly termed a theory – and what, until confirmed by the necessary evidence, it might be still more preferable to call a hypothesis – was described in a somewhat bewildering tempo, first as a doctrine and, then, a principle of international law.'

As an example of this 'bewildering tempo', Schwarzenberger cited the changing description, in successive editions of Oppenheimer's *International Law*, of a particular issue: the rule against diversion of traversing rivers. In the second edition (1912), the duty of non-interference 'is treated as based on a rule of international law to this effect'. This remained so until the fifth edition (1937), without seeking to link it to the 'still controversial doctrine' of abuse of right, but from the sixth edition (1947) onward, the duty was said to be based on the 'principle of abuse of right', even though that concept was described as a 'still controversial doctrine'.

Hersch Lauterpacht, like Schwarzenberger a permanent exile in England (the former from East Galicia, in what is now Ukraine; the latter arriving a decade later in 1933 from Germany), in the meantime had become the editor of the Oppenheim treatise. He is frequently associated with Politis as the second prominent proponent of bestowing normative effect on the concept of abuse of right (and having the advantage of writing in English). A giant in the field of international law, Lauterpacht rose to great distinction as an academic at the London School of Economics and the University of Cambridge, and later still as a Judge and President of the International Court of Justice (1955–60). One of his early works, *The Function of International Law in the International Community* (1933), contains a twenty-page chapter 14, entitled 'The Doctrine of Abuse of Right as an Instrument of Change', which commences with this sentence: 'Although as yet unknown in text-books of international law, the doctrine of abuse of right has recently attracted the attention of international lawyers.' This passage ends with a footnote in which Politis is the dominant reference.[6]

Like Politis, Lauterpacht was not seeking to elucidate the concept of abuse of right, but to enlist the theory, as the very title of his chapter revealed, as an 'instrument of change'. There is an abuse of right, he wrote in the first paragraph, 'each time the general interest of the community is

---

[6] H. Lauterpacht, *The Function of International Law in the International Community* (Oxford: Clarendon Press, 1933), p. 285.

injuriously affected as the result of the sacrifice of an important social or individual interest to a less important, though hitherto legally recognized, individual right'.

The audacity of the claim that 'legally recognized' rights should be displaced whenever they consist of a 'less important ... individual right' of single states that might harm 'the general interest of the community' becomes clear when one considers *who should make that determination*, as to which Lauterpacht's answer was clear: judges.

Moreover, like Politis, Lauterpacht perceived that the right whose abuse is in question was nothing less than sovereignty itself. He quoted Hyde with approval to the effect that 'the society of nations may at any time conclude that acts which an individual State was previously deemed to possess to commit without external interference, are so injurious to the world at large as to justify the imposition of fresh restrictions'.

There can be no doubt that his book, begun when he had just reached the age of thirty, was one of towering ambition, and has influenced successive generations until today. It constituted a broad attack on the conventional notion that international law was inapt to deal with 'non-justiciable' issues with respect to which state sovereignty could not be questioned.

This is how Lauterpacht saw the potential role of the prohibition of abuse of right: 'in international society, in which there is no authoritative legislative machinery adapting the law to changed conditions, there may be both frequent occasion and imperative necessity *for the judicial creation of new torts* through the express or implied recognition of a principle postulating the prohibition of abuse of rights'.[7]

His goal, as announced in the beginning of the chapter, may have been lofty, but Lauterpacht's attempt in the remaining pages to find support in positive law for abuse of right as such an 'instrument of change' was unimpressive.

He began with the 'practice of international tribunals', where he was able to do little more than to observe their acknowledgment of the notion that rights are lost if invoked to make extreme claims. He quoted caveats to that effect expressed by the Permanent Court of International Justice in cases where, in fact, there was no finding of abuse of right. He also referred to cases involving the sovereign rights of states to expel aliens

---

[7] Lauterpacht, *The Function of International Law in the International Community*, p. 287. Emphasis added.

from their territory, which some international tribunals had said could trigger responsibility under international law in the event the foreigner had been allowed entry and no justification was given for the expulsion. Why this must be viewed as an abuse of right is unclear, since the more straightforward proposition is that the act of *admission* of aliens may be associated with some obligations as to their treatment. The same observation may be made with respect to the right to close ports to foreign commerce, which were viewed as associated with the duty under international law 'to give notice to those regularly admitted'.

At any rate, Lauterpacht was transparent about his embrace of what he deemed to be natural law as 'a lever of progress'. He later wrote: 'The law of nature has been rightly exposed to the charge of vagueness and arbitrariness. But the uncertainty of the "higher law" is preferable to the arbitrariness and insolence of naked force.'[8]

This was plainly not an attempt to state the law but a call to arms to change it. It can hardly be said, as we shall see in the next chapter, that the international community of states showed much eagerness to accept the suggested expansion of adjudicatory authority.

---

[8] H. Lauterpacht, 'The Grotian Tradition in International Law', 23 *British Yearbook of International Law* (1946), 1–53.

The Politis/Lauterpacht project foundered both on academic rejection and (above all) the jealousy of states with regard to their sovereignty. The pragmatic alternative was first described by Kiss in a remarkable doctoral thesis in 1953, prefaced by five incisive words by Bastid, his supervisor: 'it [abuse of right] should not be taken literally'. In this more modest conception, the prevention of abuse of right (which no one will dispute as an abstract proposition) is recognized as a general policy goal, requiring the hard work of negotiating contextually meaningful criteria as lex specialis. This reasonable retrenchment is informed by the understanding that avoiding abuse of rights on the international plane requires the accommodation of concurrent rights which may naturally generate competing claims. This process does not call for the assignment of moral blame, and cannot succeed as intuitive projections of the phrase 'abuse of right'.

7

Rejection and Retrenchment

The attempt to elevate the notion of abuse of right to the status of an internationally recognised general principle of law faltered in two stages. First came the simple recognition that the project could not generate a consensus in its favour. Realists thereafter retreated to a more modest strategy – namely, to pursue the objective of curtailing excessive claims of right as a policy objective by *promoting specific treaty commitments having that effect*, which was a very different objective than seeking acceptance of a general commanding principle. This chapter begins by examining the absence of consensus around the quest for recognition of a general principle and then explores the approach taken by pragmatists who saw that something of value might nevertheless be pursued in another, less quixotic way.

The Hostile Reception

Responding in 1956 to Lauterpacht's thesis that the indeterminateness of 'higher law' is preferable to 'the arbitrariness of the insolence of naked power',[1] Georg Schwarzenberger – Lauterpacht's academic adversary in more ways than one – was harsh and hostile, as reflected in the passage

---

[1] H. Lauterpacht, 'The Grotian Tradition in International Law', 23 *British Yearbook of International Law* (1946), 1–53.

85

quoted in Chapter 6.[2] Almost a decade earlier, in a *Harvard Law Review* article where he criticised the approach taken by Lauterpacht in *Oppenheim's International Law,* he had railed against those who

> appear to pick and choose from natural and positive law exactly as they think fit ... [deciding] with an air of infallibility what God and Reason ordain, and state practice is usually more honored by neglect than by systematic study. Mutual quotation clubs and what Bentham called 'ipse-dixitism' became rampant in the treatment of international law.[3]

Specifically with respect to the notion of abuse of right, no less a figure than Gerald Fitzmaurice affirmed that 'the doctrine cannot be regarded as definitively established, or as constituting an accepted principle of international law'.[4] J. L. Brierly's classic textbook *The Law of Nations,* the sixth edition of which was edited by Humphrey Waldock in 1963, did not mention the expression.

As for Schwarzenberger (who naturally agreed with Fitzmaurice), his sustained attack on the 'hypothesis' of abuse of right in his aforementioned Grotius Society speech was sarcastic:

> Why engage in painstaking research work if the desired result can be attained by way of asserting that the prohibition of abuse of rights is a general principle of law recognized by civilized nations? ... The apparent shortcut of attempting to prove that the prohibition of abuse of rights is a general principle ... proves to be full of snares. ... Yet, be it assumed that, in a particular system of municipal law, the notion of the prohibition of abuse of rights has exercised a formative influence on the creation of actual rules of law. This would hardly constitute evidence that such an evolutionary principle behind the law was a regulative principle *de lege lata,* and an overriding principle into the bargain.[5]

This is not the place for an account of Schwarzenberger's lengthy demonstration; the point is only to underline the controversial nature of the proposition that the notion of abuse of right could generate an acknowledged rule of decision. A few passages, among dozens, should suffice:

---

[2] G. Schwarzenberger, 'Uses and Abuses of the "Abuse of Rights" in International Law', 42 *Transactions of the Grotius Society* (1956), 147–79.

[3] G. Schwarzenberger, 'The Inductive Approach to International Law', 60 *Harvard Law Review* (1947), 539, at 544–5.

[4] G. Fitzmaurice, 'The Law and Procedure of the International Court of Justice: General Principles and Substantive Law', 27 *British Yearbook of International Law* (1950), 1, at 12 and 14, n. 14.

[5] Schwarzenberger, 'Uses and Abuses of the "Abuse of Rights" in International Law', 149–50.

Once it is examined critically within what confines it is really necessary to pray in aid the hypothesis of abuse of rights as a regulative factor, a surprising number of fields emerge in which this appears redundant or outright misleading. . . .

[W]hen the operation of rules underlying the principle of sovereignty is excluded or limited by other rules of international law, this hypothesis [of abuse of right] is redundant. . . . Although the prohibition of abuse of rights is not the real reason of the illegality of the act in question, the illustration serves its appointed purpose of turning another piece of 'incontrovertible' evidence of the doctrine. . . . Especially when alleged rights are exercised surreptitiously or deceitfully, the typical reason is that one of the facts which constituted one of the conditions of the exercise of a right does not actually exist. It, therefore, must be manufactured in order to take the act out of the operative field of another rule of international law. Again, it is redundant first to imagine the existence of a right and then to devise, like a *deus ex machina*, its abuse and the prohibition thereto. All that is required is to ignore the pretence and to deal with the case on its rue facts. Then, the misrepresentation and the bad faith implicit in it are merely relevant in order to provide conclusive evidence that the case in question falls under the rule which it was the purpose of the façade erected to evade.[6]

Bin Cheng himself, as must be emphasised at every turn to ensure that the wrong conclusion is not drawn from the fact that the passages relating to abuse of right appear in a book entitled *General Principles*, never endorsed the notion even as a principle, let alone as a rule of decision; there is to the contrary every reason to believe that he shared Schwarzenberger's doubts (if not his vehemence). Cheng referred to abuse of right as a 'theory'. In so doing, he was faithful not only to Politis, but also to Schwarzenberger, who as seen remarked on Politis's prudence in this regard.[7] In his Grotius Society speech, Schwarzenberger had observed that the reasoning of actual decisions of international courts and tribunals 'hardly bears out the hypothesis of a prohibition of abuse of rights, and that any true answer will depend on more painstaking forms of inductive research'.

Schwarzenberger's earlier Harvard article in 1947 was precisely entitled 'The Inductive Approach to International Law'. In that substantial essay, he excoriated what he called the 'eclectic approach to international law', whose practitioners 'appear to pick and choose from natural and positive law exactly as they think fit'[8] and was unsparing of Lauterpacht's work in the *Oppenheim* treatise. He sought to 'call away from the dreamland of deductive speculation to the reality of hard work on raw material waiting

[6] Schwarzenberger, 'Uses and Abuses of the "Abuse of Rights" in International Law', 153–5.
[7] See Chapter 6, note 5.
[8] Schwarzenberger, 'The Inductive Approach to International Law', 544.

for the workman' prepared to 'grapple seriously with the systematic pre-
sentation of the practice of individual states'. Schwarzenberger was, in fact,
Cheng's mentor; he had suggested the subject of *General Principles*, supervised the study, and written the foreword. The second sentence of Cheng's
introduction, on page one of the book, begins with the declaration 'The
present work is an attempt to apply the inductive method', referring to
Schwarzenberger's Harvard article.[9] The nail in the coffin is this: Cheng's
elogious preface to Roulet's book-length dismissal of abuse of right as
a general principle was explicitly agnostic as to 'the place of the theory of
abuse of rights in international law'.

Above all, the international community of states has never embraced
the radical instrumentalist vision of abuse of rights advanced by Politis
and Lauterpacht. The fact that idealistic scholarly writings are pleasing to
other scholars does not count for much when contradicted by the reality
of state practice. There is little authority in the exhortations of what
Schwarzenberger called 'mutual quotation clubs'. In one of the most
prominent works on the history of the period between the two world
wars (still widely read today), E. H. Carr wrote the following:

> No government was willing to entrust to an international court the power to
> modify its legal rights. Some theorists, however, were more ready than
> practical statesmen to brush this difficulty aside, and were quite prepared to
> entrust to a so-called arbitral tribunal the task not only of applying existing
> rights, but of creating new ones. . . . Professor Lauterpacht [believed] that
> international conflicts of interest are due . . . to the imperfections of inter-
> national legal organisation. . . . It is a pity that Professor Lauterpacht, having
> brilliantly conducted his analysis up to the point where the unwillingness of
> States is recognized as the limiting factor in the justiciability of international
> disputes, should not have been content to leave it there, treating this
> 'unwillingness', in *true utopian fashion*, as perverse and underserving of
> the attention of an international lawyer. . . . It may not be that men stupidly
> or wickedly failed to apply right principles, but that *the principles themselves
> were false and inapplicable.*[10]

---

[9] Decades later, Cheng co-edited the *liber amicorum* in his mentor's honour. See B. Cheng
and E. D. Brown (eds.), *Contemporary Problems of International Law: Essays in Honours
of Georg Schwarzenberger* (Stevens & Sons, 1988).

[10] E. H. Carr, *The Twenty Years' Crisis 1919–1939* (Harper Perennial, 1964), p. 249 and 39 (still
in print, reissued with a new introduction in 2001; emphasis added). The internal quotation is
to H. Lauterpacht, *The Function of Law in the International Community* (Oxford, 1933), p.
249. Carr served as a diplomat in the Foreign Office for twenty years before embarking on
a prolific academic career, assuming the Woodrow Wilson Chair of International Politics at
the University College of Wales in 1936. The fact that his left-wing realist views were
controversial is immaterial to the point being made. When the University of Chicago

The international community of states was not eager to accept the expansion of adjudicatory authority desired by Politis and Lauterpacht. As seen, both Politis and Lauterpacht were prudent in the characterisation of the concept of abuse of right and did not declare its prohibition to be a principle.[11] This was left to their followers. But by the 1950s, faced with the failure of abuse of rights to attain the status of a principle of law, more realistic voices came to the fore.

Retrenchment

Having encountered the persistence of serious doctrinal resistance, and even more adamant obduracy on the part of states, the realists saw that there was no way the concept could generate consensus in its favour and thereafter lowered their aim: to promote the notion of abuse of right as a consideration that might inspire even exclusively self-interested states *to make voluntary accommodations, in particular by treaty.* Unfortunately these realists have created considerable confusion because of their continued use of the expression abuse of right, even though they were not proposing an autonomous rule of decision, but rather a way of describing the effect of the kinds of international agreements they sought to encourage.

This realists' move crystallised in a book written by Alexandre Kiss – and in five words written by Suzanne Bastid in 1953. Kiss had emigrated from Hungary to France in 1947 at the age of twenty-two, and six years later published *L'abus de droit en droit international,* one of the most important studies of the subject, read and cited by all scholars who have paid sustained

---

Professor John Mearsheimer gave the E. H. Carr Memorial Lecture in 2004, he immediately stated that 'the core arguments that Carr laid out in *The Twenty Years' Crisis* are as relevant today as they were in the dark decade of the 1930s. . . . Carr, I think, would be appalled by the almost complete absence of realists and the near total dominance of idealists in the contemporary British academy'. See J. Mearsheimer, 'E. H. Carr vs. Idealism: The Battle Rages On', 19(2) *International Relations* (2005), 139–40.

[11] Although the prospective impact of the doctrine of abuse of right conceived by Lauterpacht turned out to be unrealistic, it was unfair for Carr in 1964 to dismiss Lauterpacht as a 'true utopian'. In the 5th edition of *Oppenheim,* which appeared in 1935, Lauterpacht had warned scholars of the danger of advancing too far ahead of state officials. The development of international law, he wrote on page 517, came through state practice, 'by common action of the States themselves, and not by jurists engaged in drawing logical consequences' from the Paris Peace Pact of 1928 (more portentously named the General Pact for the Renunciation of War, also known as the Kellogg-Briand Treaty), which was notably signed by Japan and Italy, two States that by the time Lauterpacht wrote those lines had launched wars of aggression against China and Ethiopia – and even darker clouds were amassing; Germany was also a signatory.

attention to the topic. This was Kiss's doctoral thesis, recognised immediately as a work of exceptional merit and published by the French *Centre national de recherche scientifique*.[12] Bastid, already a formidable presence among French scholars (and later to become the first woman to sit on the International Court of Justice, as an ad hoc judge in *Libya* v. *Tunisia*), had taken the young scholar under her wings and supervised his thesis.

In her glowing preface to his book, Bastid could not resist pointing out that the attempt to incorporate the notion of *abus de droit* into the international context revealed that the expression should not be 'taken literally', given that in this environment the search for principles have a different aim – namely to restrict the exercise of state authority (which she referred to as *competences*). This is what she wrote:

> Although the expression *abus de droit* is frequently used in a number of decisions applying international law, it *should not be taken literally*. Mr Kiss demonstrates very well that the subject in fact pertains to the conditions under which international law acknowledges the exercise of State authority; all authority implies duties to act as well as freedom of action.[13]

Bastid praised Kiss for his meticulous identification of three forms of abuse of right, each being abuses of authority: acts of a state to interfere in the internal legal order of another state, *détournement de pouvoir* (misuse of power), and arbitrary acts of authority. She also acknowledged that the importance of a state's authority 'for maintaining its cohesion as an entity' and 'the absence of organized systematic control' provide explanations for 'the complexities and the contradictions of international practice'.[14] She might as well have said that 'we are a long way from Politis's dream'.

Kiss himself harboured no illusions, using terms that Schwarzenberger would have applauded: 'until now the literature of international law has concerned itself more with deduction than demonstration, and the number of cases examined from this point of view is highly limited; in truth the point of view *de lege ferenda* has so far taken precedence over the study of precedents'.[15] He referred to 'a difficulty which we shall face at every step; is the position taken by a government contrary to a rule of international law, or is it rejected only because we deem it to be an *exces de pouvoir* or an abuse of right?'[16]

---

[12] A. Kiss, *L'abus de droit en droit international* (Pichon & Durand-Auzias, 1953).
[13] Kiss, *L'abus de droit en droit international*, p. 5.
[14] Kiss, *L'abus de droit en droit international*, p. 6.
[15] Kiss, *L'abus de droit en droit international*, p. 12.
[16] Kiss, *L'abus de droit en droit international*, p. 13.

What then to do? Kiss's answer was to explain how states might see the advantage of avoiding 'abusive' conduct *by other states* and therefore find it tolerable to accept limitations on their own authority. For this, of course, one needs no notion of 'abuse of right' as an autonomous general principle, since the idea is to achieve the goal by negotiating treaties, at the highest level of the normative hierarchy of Article 38 of the Statute of the International Court of Justice. It would require no principle even if one existed – and that is why Bastid said, 'Do not take it literally.'

She was impressed enough by one of Kiss's examples of how this might work that she referred to it in her preface – namely, the authority given by the States who had formed the new European Coal and Steel Community to its Court of Justice, vesting power to sanction abuse of power and conduct (or failure to act) causing 'fundamental and persistent harm' to the economy of another state, and noted that even private enterprises would have standing to seize the court if affected by harmful state conduct. Kiss himself gave detailed and fascinating accounts of how the 'sovereign States' of the United States and the 'sovereign Cantons' of the Swiss Confederation could be ordered to conduct themselves as riparians so as not to harm their 'sovereign' neighbours.

But, of course, this presupposes prior agreement, in the particular instances just cited taking the solid form of *constitutions* of a permanent and existential nature that give plenary authority to a federal supreme court. From the perspective of the 1950s, the 'sovereign relations' among such confederated states, or among West European states, were immensely different from the relations among the sovereign states of the First, Second, and Third Worlds. And our present world community still does not resemble Switzerland.

The world community of states is, in sum, a different universe than that of private citizens of single, comprehensive legal systems testing the limits of rights bestowed upon them by sovereigns. We are considering the self-imposed restrictions on sovereigns when they act pursuant to self-declared authority. Such restrictions – now advancing, now retreating – may not evolve fast enough to satisfy us, in a fragmented international environment where the community and system are only aspirational. But it is what we have, and it works only in this modest and painstaking way.

To take a single example: if a treaty (such as the 1997 UN Convention on the Law of the Non-navigational Uses of International Watercourses) recognises a duty that may impinge on the pursuit of purely national interests (such as the obligation to have regard to vital human needs in the event of a conflict between possible uses of rivers), it makes no sense, in the event this duty is found to have been neglected, to speak of an abuse of sovereign right, since the straightforward proposition is that the treaty has been breached. This is a matter of positive international law, whatever one might think of the lack of specificity of the particular duty in question.[17] In the example given, the Treaty was accompanied by Statements of Understanding that added some measure of concreteness to this provision: 'in determining "vital human needs", special attention is to be paid to providing sufficient water to sustain human life, including both drinking water and water required for food in order to prevent starvation'.[18]

Some activists and scholars put little stock in treaties, which they consider to be negotiated by diplomats looking only to the short-term interests of their particular governments, without appreciating the imperatives of the long-term welfare of the international community. They are prepared to invoke the 'principle of abuse of right' as a shortcut to justify law-making by judges and arbitrators. And so the expression lives on.

Nearly two decades after the publication of *L'abus de droit en droit international,* G. D. S. Taylor considered Kiss's approach in an article published in the *British Yearbook,* lauding its 'most thorough investigation of abuse of rights'. Noting Kiss's 'three headings' of such wrongdoing, Taylor perhaps inadvertently poured a good measure of cold water on Kiss's project by noting that his second category (use of a conferred power in contradiction with its purpose), although conceptually having the greatest potential ambit and 'scope for growth', is also the least likely to bite for a simple reason: 'Few State powers are conferred.'[19] (A rare example is the right conferred by the United Nations to govern a territory under a trusteeship mandate, as we shall see in Chapter 8.)

Kiss went on to academic prominence at the Robert Schuman University in Strasbourg. Considered a pioneer in the field of international environmental law (indeed by some as its father, having published general treatises on the subject in the mid-1970s), he was a scholar-

---

[17] UN Convention on the Law of the Non-Navigational Uses of International Watercourses, New York, 21 May 1997, 36 ILM (1999), 700.
[18] UN Convention on the Law of the Non-Navigational Uses of International Watercourses, New York, 21 May 1997, 36 ILM (1999), 719.
[19] G. D. S. Taylor, 'The Content of the Rule Against Abuse of Rights in International Law', 46 *British Yearbook of International Law* (1972–3), 323.

activist who served as president of the European Council for Environmental Law.[20]

Given the subject of his well-known first book half a century earlier, it was hardly surprising that Kiss was asked to update the entry on 'abuse of rights' in the Max Planck *Encyclopedia of Public International Law* in 2006, shortly before his death. His contribution referred to the *concept* of abuse of right as being inspired by a *principle* of Roman law. Two sentences appeared as follows: 'On the whole *it may be considered* that international law prohibits the abuse of rights. However, such prohibition *does not seem* to be unanimously accepted in general international law, while it is not contested in the law of international institutions.'[21] After referring to the unremarkable fact that international courts and tribunals have '*examined* the way in which a State exercised a right', a fairly clear indication of the absence of a precedent *applying* abuse of right as a rule of decision, he went on in the following inconclusive (some might say agnostic) way: 'Dissenting opinions of judges at the PCIJ and the ICJ have frequently adverted to the principle, but some of them expressed hesitation before applying it, without rejecting outright its place in international law.'[22]

Those who nevertheless believe in the usefulness of 'abuse of right' admit, as they must, that its effect is limited to having a 'corrective' effect, to save the day when a decision-maker finds that it must never have occurred to the legislator that a right might be used in an unexpected way that, in the name of justice, cannot be tolerated.[23]

---

[20] He was also a member of Hungary's counsel team in the *Gabčíkovo–Nagyonmaros* case at the ICJ, one of the most prominent international disputes involving environmental issues. See *Gabčíkovo-Nagymaros Project (Hungary v. Slovakia)*, judgment, 25 September 1997, *I.C.J. Reports* (1997), 7.

[21] A. Kiss, 'Abuse of Rights', in R. Wolfrum (ed.), *Max Planck Encyclopedia of Public International Law* (Oxford University Press, 2006), para. 7.

[22] He added that the 'clearest jurisdictional formulation of the norm prohibiting abuse of right' was that of the WTO Appellate Body in *United States - Import Prohibition of Certain Shrimp and Shrimp Products*, WT/DS58/AB/R, report of the Appellate Body, 12 October 1998, citing a passage that is hardly clear at all; it states that 'the doctrine of *abus de droit* prohibits the abusive exercise of a state's rights and enjoins that whenever the assertion of a right "impinges on the field covered by [a] treaty obligation, it must be exercised bona fide..."' (Kiss, 'Abuse of Rights', para. 14). This is, in fact, an unremarkable example of the implication of the undoubted general principle of good faith; the words *abus de droit* add nothing.

[23] A. Pirovano, 'La fonction sociale des droits: Réflexions sur le destin des théories de Josserand', 13 *Recueil Dalloz-Sirey Chronique* (1972), 67, wrote that '*la théorie de l'abus de droit ... est un mécanisme correcteur qui permet au juge d'assouplir le jeu des relations*

It is interesting to consider how this proposition squares with certain issues that have come up in relation to the bilateral investment treaties ('BITs'), which have given rise to a multitude of arbitrations against states in the past three decades. In the case of BITs, the 'legislator' is of course the relevant set of treaty negotiators. They may say (as they have indeed done in a few treaties) that an investment must be specifically approved in each case to be entitled to benefit from the treaty. They may also include (as has also been done) a so-called denial of benefits clause, which excludes shell companies by providing that a corporate entity may not invoke the treaty unless they have a significant presence in the country of their incorporation.

But how about the admissibility of a BIT claim that has already been the subject of a 'notice of dispute' communicated to the host state by another entity? It is common that international investments may involve more than one entity in the same corporate chain, and that each of them may have claims of different dimensions that arise from the same governmental acts. That the government may reach a settlement with one entity, after it is no longer in the same corporate chain, but not the other, is an obvious possibility. No treaty forbids the pursuit of the surviving claim, nor does such a prohibition seem to be required in the interests of justice. To the contrary, injustice would result if the government colludes with one of the entities to reduce the former's overall liability. There is no reason to 'correct the law'. In fact, it would be a usurpation of law-making authority.[24] If states party to BITs wanted things to work this way, they would have so stipulated.[25] They evidently either do not, or have not perceived it as something that needs to be excluded.

> *juridiques'* ('the theory of abuse of right . . . is a corrective mechanism, a safety valve that allows the judge to accommodate the interplay of legal relationships').
>
> [24] In the conclusion of her article – E. Reid, 'Abuse of Rights in Scots Law', 2 *Edinburg Law Review* (1998), 129 – Professor Reid refers at page 157 to cases from France and Quebec as suggesting that the 'doctrine' of abuse of right is being used as 'a tool of judicial law-making with which new areas of liability may be marked out'. This is startling enough as a proposition in France, where there is no law of precedent. (Since it first appeared more than two centuries ago, the *Code civil* provides, in the simple words of Article 5, that 'judges are forbidden from pronouncing judgments in the form of general or regulatory rules'). In the context of ICSID, where arbitrators are not allowed to create law, it is shocking. The last words of Pirovano's article cited in note 23 were these: 'one cannot fault judges for doing what the State itself has been incapable of doing; society as a whole must decide the purpose of rights a priori, and not judges a posteriori . . . the notion of abuse of right leads inevitably to a matter of public policy'. To paraphrase, the states signatory to BITs would certainly reject in the most categorical terms that an ICSID arbitral tribunal would either define or limit rights in their place.
>
> [25] One recalls the example of the Czech Republic in the well-known *CME/Lauder* cases, where CME and Mr Lauder as shareholders in the affected investment offered to proceed

It is easy to agree that conduct considered to be an abuse of right should not be condoned. But as a supposed rule, this leads to irremediable unpredictability (and thus arbitrariness), since there are infinite opinions as to the factors that make conduct abusive. Let us consider only a few examples. Is malice necessary, or is disproportionality between the right asserted and the harm caused enough? Indeed, is it not the case that all respondents may consider that the enforcement of ordinary contractual rights inflicts 'harm' on them because the application of the terms of the contract has become disadvantageous? What is one to make of a claim that a right is not being used for its intended purpose, if 'purpose' is necessarily left to the eye of the beholder? Studying cases and commentaries, we have seen that it takes no great effort to put forward thirty-four inconsistent subjective formulations of abuse of right (see Chapter 3). This disqualifies it as rule of decision. An adequate rule can be generated only by a *lex specialis* that defines the abuse of the rights it creates by reference to circumstances established by law, whether a statute or a treaty, or explicitly accords adjudicatory discretion in a particular respect where it seems appropriate.

Conceivably a rule of decision established by an unusually rigorous and stable *jurisprudence constante,* untouched by statutes or treaties for a significant period of time, could also operate as such a *lex specialis*, but it seems wholly unlikely that this will occur at the international level, and the judicial hesitations and contradictions within individual national legal systems do not show much promise there either.

Whatever sympathy one may have for the idealistic impulses of its proponents, the notion of abuse of right cannot be the foundation for a general principle of law or an acceptable rule of decision. As an *analytical matter*, the conclusion that there has been an abuse of right is either redundant because the claim is invalid under other rules of decision, or else depends on the personal proclivities of the decision-maker. As a *matter of policy*, and of special concern in the field of international law, decisions that result in individual case-by-case rule-making by adjudicatory bodies often weaken general adherence to the law.

The only place for the notion of abuse of right is therefore when the law-maker determines that a certain type of right may generate

in consolidated arbitrations but the state insisted on two distinct arbitrations. See *CME Czech Republic B.V.* v. *The Czech Republic*, UNCITRAL, partial award, 13 September 2001; final award, 14 March 2003; *Ronald S. Lauder* v. *The Czech Republic*, UNCITRAL, final award, 3 September 2001.

temptations to abuse in ways that are difficult to define, and therefore justify an explicit *legislated* grant of adjudicatory discretion (e.g., in the form of authority to decide on the basis of equitable considerations), either broadly or with specifically tailored guidelines. When such discretion is granted, decision-makers would add only confusion by invoking the nebulous expression 'abuse of right'; they need only look to the grant of discretion. There seems to be no BIT that contains such a grant of discretion, and – given the specific jurisdictional requirements that such treaties contain – it would take an unacceptable degree of hubris on the part of arbitrators to purport to expand or restrict those criteria on the basis of their own preferences. This point is powerfully confirmed by the fact that some states have amended BITs to include specific waivers designed to prevent parallel proceedings. Such provisions reveal the understanding of those states that the desired result required a treaty amendment, which a priori is inapplicable to an investor entitled to invoke the original text. If and when applicable, such a provision is designed to be analysed and applied with specificity, not discretion, on the part of the tribunal.

But the persistent use of the term 'abuse of right' – and the fact that everyone rejects 'abuse' in the abstract – has left unfortunate confusion between the concrete prevention of perceived abuses of rights through explicit rules of international law and the autonomous operation of an overarching normative principle. This confusion is made even worse by the innumerable uses of the single word 'abuse' in other contexts, such as abuse of process and abuse of corporate forms for tax avoidance – and, in the international sphere, such examples as the abusive alteration of exchange rates or other manipulations of money, abusive use of the freedom of use of the high seas (e.g., in laying cables), and abusive activities of upstream riparians. Such uses of the single word cannot be said to have anything to do with the exercise of 'rights' save by intellectual contortions of the kind that Schwarzenberger deplored.[26] The expression 'abuse of process', which does not, except in the most artificial sense, involve the misuse of any right, is probably the greatest source of incoherence. For example, there is no reason to say that a party that makes an *oppressive* demand for documents of the other side is engaging in abuse of the process of discovery. The rejection of oppressive demands is an *inherent limitation* of a procedural opportunity, and does not require the sterile intellectual circularity of being called an abuse of the right of access

---

[26] See the quotation in note 5.

to documents that would have been provided if the request had not been oppressive.

Another example will serve to conclude this part. In 1998, the Appellate Body of the World Trade Organization notably invoked *abus de droit* in the *Shrimp-Turtle* case, using the French expression untranslated. Answering the argument of the United States that its alteration of rules for foreign fishing was permissible under Article XX(g) of the General Agreement on Tariffs and Trade, which creates an exception for 'the conservation of exhaustible natural resources', the Appellate Body wrote:

> [T]he application widely known as the doctrine of *abus de droit* prohibits the abusive exercise of a state's rights and enjoins that whenever the assertion of right 'impinges on a field covered by [a] treaty obligation, it must be exercised bona fide, that is to say, reasonably'. An abusive exercise by a Member of its own treaty right thus results in a breach of the treaty rights of the other Members and, as well, a violation of the treaty obligations of the member so acting.[27]

Having said that, the Appellate Body then announced that it was faced with the 'delicate' task of 'locating and marking out a line of equilibrium between the right of a Member to invoke an . . . exception and the rights of the other Members under varying substantive provisions'.[28]

This nod to the 'doctrine' of abuse of rights is scarcely proof of the normative force of the expression, because the phrase *abuse of right* does not tell us by what standards the 'delicate' determination of a 'line of equilibrium' would take place. Nevertheless, the Canadian academic Michael Byers, in a lengthy article in 2002 entitled 'Abuse of Rights: An Old Principle, A New Age', heralded this decision as support for his contention that abuse of rights 'may be a deft instrument . . . in dealing with issues such as transboundary pollution, declining fishstocks and whale populations, and the protection of areas such as the Antarctic and space'.[29]

These are the very issues that were Kiss's life work as a pioneer of international environmental law.[30] As we have seen this domain does not

---

[27] *United States – Import Prohibition of Certain Shrimp and Shrimp Products*, WT/DS58/AB/R, report of the Appellate Body, 12 October 1998, at para. 158.

[28] *United States – Import Prohibition of Certain Shrimp and Shrimp Products*, WT/DS58/AB/R, report of the Appellate Body, 12 October 1998, at para. 159.

[29] M. Byers, 'Abuse of Rights: An Old Principle, A New Age', 47 *McGill Law Journal* (2002), 389.

[30] Byers himself, a young law school professor when he wrote his article, subsequently joined the Department of Political Science at the University of British Columbia to focus

really raise issues of abuse at all, but of the collision of rights – or, to put it more constructively, the resolution of defensible competing claims. In this context, one may well consider that it is abusive to insist on the right of one person or entity without regard to the effect of its exercise on rights of others, but – and here is what is important – the result should be to pursue the objective of accommodating, reconciling, or adjusting all concurrent rights by way of context-specific solutions, rather than assuming that adjudicators have the authority to establish 'the equilibrium' as they see fit. Even when states act in contravention of international law, their representatives are seeking to promote the public interest of their citizens as they see it; it is one thing for an international court to hold that they would thereby exceed legal bounds, and quite another to castigate them as engaged in abuse.

A Critique of Robert Kolb's 'Polymorph Galaxy'

The 265 pages of Robert Kolb's important monograph *Good Faith in International Law*[31] contain a 12-page section entitled 'Good Faith and the Prohibition of Abuse of Rights'. We have already seen, in the final part of Chapter 2, that the prohibition in question is not a necessary corollary of good faith and was therefore not an indispensable part of his work. Fair enough – one might consider that the unnecessary connection is so often made that it was natural to devote some attention to it. But the book endorses the status of the prohibition as a general principle of international law, which is contrary to the thesis of the present study. Here is why.

Kolb's proceeds in two steps. First, he counters a number of objections to the conclusion that the prohibition is a general principle, and then he makes his positive case.

The first of the objections he seeks to overcome is what he calls 'the logomachy argument', although he does not trace it to its original source, namely the famous and routinely quoted passage from Planiol – reproduced and discussed in the second part of Chapter 2 – 'if I use my right, my act is licit; and when it is illicit it is because I exceed my right and act without right'. (In this context, we may consider 'logomachy' to be synonymous with 'oxymoron'.) In any event, Kolb is peremptory and

---

prominently on issues concerning outer space, sovereignty in the Arctic, climate change, and the law of the sea.

[31] Kolb, *Good Faith in International Law* (Hart Publishing, 2017).

dismissive: 'The argument is not convincing.'[32] But let us examine the rationale he advances in support of this assertion.

Kolb suggests that the core issue is the need to find a solution when the exercise of a right exceeds its desirable limits but the law has not defined them. The choice is then between embracing the principle of abuse of right to establish those limits or considering the matter to be one of interpreting the effect of a right that has been imperfectly defined. Adjudicators who follow the first path declare that the right must be limited; if they prefer the second they affirm that certain actions are not part of the right. Either way, the decision is made 'on the basis of considerations which are in both cases rooted in reasonableness and non-abuse'. This equiparation is itself questionable, but that perhaps does not matter, because the important issue then becomes which option is to be preferred (interpretation versus recourse to a rule of prohibition of abuse of rights).

Kolb prefers recognition of an abuse-of-right rule because he finds it 'more prudent' and 'restrictive' than the interpretive route since 'the right of the state is not affected and only a particular exercise of the right is condemned'. Interpreting the text that defines the right, on the other hand, 'may often have a larger scope by denying the availability of the right in its entirety'. The argument seems vulnerable to at least three formidable objections. First, an adjudicator interpreting the text defining a right in such a way as to limit it should surely have sufficient confidence in that conclusion to assume responsibility for holding his or her inter-pretation to be generally valid. Second, that adjudicator in any event does not have universal authority, and does not bind another decision-maker. Third, and above all, a finding of abuse of right is surely a very serious matter and very likely to offend the party (perhaps a powerful state) held to have adopted an abusive position. It could result (as has happened on many occasions) in harsh condemnations of international law and the international institutions charged with applying it. This can hardly be less

---

[32] Kolb, *Good Faith in International Law*, p. 137. Professor Chris Brunner, in C. Brunner, 'Abuse of Rights in Dutch Law', 37 *Louisiana Law Review* (1977), 729, credited his colleague F. G. Scheltema with a logical, if only partial, refutation of Planiol's phrase; it is not *necessarily* correct because if the consequences the law attaches to the unacceptable conduct is only the payment of damages, one might conclude that a price was paid for the excessive exercise of a right; 'the abuse ... would not be equivalent to acting without right'. Still, Brunner observed, 'A survey of cases concerning abuse of right shows convincingly that Dutch courts deal with abuse of right as a behavior without right.' See Brunner, 'Abuse of Rights in Dutch Law', 729.

sensitive than being told that the right does not extend as far as that party thought.

Moreover, whatever one makes of the choice between the solution of interpretation and that of applying the prohibition against the abuse of right, it does not seem to make a dent in Planiol's observation that the second alternative involves the oxymoron that you are not entitled to a right which you do not have.

But Kolb presents a second argument, based on the need to fill gaps that leave particular conduct to be 'neither permitted nor prohibited'. In such cases, he posits, the adjudicator (he uses the words 'legal operator') needs to have recourse to the doctrine of abuse of right or to some equivalent principle, and thus the doctrine, though perhaps 'chased by the door . . . will come back through the window' and thus the logomachy argument is 'at best circular'.

It is difficult to see how this is a refutation of Planiol's objection. If the doctrine (or anything 'equivalent to it') is enlisted to provide the solution, it is the denial of a right and therefore the establishment of its non-existence. How can this be anything but an interpretive exercise? Adjudicators who fill gaps should do so with great circumspection when deciding that the text defining the asserted right does or does not extend to the controversial action or situation. The issue is at the heart of this book; its thesis is that such matters should not be decided by giving unbridled implicit discretion to adjudicators to determine abuse. There are carefully established canons for the interpretation of treaties, not to be replaced by appeals to a facile epithet as polymorphous as abuse of rights.

After this unimpressive start, Kolb makes a number of very short arguments that – perhaps inevitably given their brevity – share the characteristic of being more in the nature of assertions than demonstrations. Most of these points are refutations of arguments that are not made by this book, and seem to be straw men of little interest. But two merit mention.

Kolb gives short shrift to the objection that the doctrine of abuse of right 'supposes a certain homogeneity of values' and 'can exist only in municipal societies'. Here, in a section comprising only two short paragraphs, he is even more dismissive – 'a truly weak argument . . . the possibility of a doctrine of abuse of rights on the level of positive law is not forestalled by such dogmatic considerations'.[33] A peremptory tone does not, however, win the day in any serious company. (One can easily

---

[33] Kolb, *Good Faith in International Law*, p. 139.

imagine Schwarzenberger's withering riposte.) For the objection is serious, and could be overcome only by a substantial effort of documenta-
tion and ratiocination which would at best only be tentative. We have
seen in Chapter 1 that the drafters of the UNIDROIT Principles, who
consciously sought to establish 'general principles' while affirming the
'irrelevance' of 'national standards', made no claims for the doctrine of
abuse of right.[34] Kolb makes the appalling mistake (one must say) of
asking this rhetorical question: 'Are there not, in international society,
elites that have often studied in the same universities and share even
a common language?' This seems a disastrous premise, comprehensively
demolished by Anthea Roberts in her book *Is International Law
International?*[35]

The remaining refutation to be dealt with here (likewise made only in
two short paragraphs) is more attractive. Kolb seeks to defuse the argument that the doctrine is useless when faced with the fact that international law 'is composed mainly of vague, flexible, indeterminate norms,
which can be interpreted in a way to avoid hardship'. He points out that
much of modern international law is 'precise and rigid', thus, it seems,
conceding that it is ever less necessary to have recourse to the doctrine in
any event. He then observes that the doctrine 'has often been considered
particularly important in the context of discretionary rights, i.e. in the
area of large and vague state powers'. It is a valid observation, and it
should lead to a conclusion that is consistent with a key proposition
clearly seen by Bastid, when she introduced her student Kiss's doctoral
thesis and wrote that abuse of right 'should not be taken literally' (see the
abstract of this chapter), and is also consistent with a recurrent theme of
this book. These are important matters that, by their nature, cannot be
encapsulated with precision and must allow for discretionary authority
by the adjudicator, who will have to rule in the light of particular
circumstances. In those situations, the law-maker cedes to the law-
applier's explicit discretion, and of course that discretion can be informed
by the objective of not allowing abuse. But this is not a warrant for
allowing international judges and arbitrators the authority to apply an
indeterminate abuse-of-rights 'rule' to rights that are not created with an
accompanying grant of adjudicatory discretion.

We now come to Kolb's affirmative argument in favour of the trans-
formation of the concept to a rule of decision, seeking to demonstrate

---

[34] See Chapter 1, note 19.
[35] A. Roberts, *Is International Law International?* (Oxford University Press, 2017).

that 'positive international law has developed that principle' in four 'contexts':[36] 'the prohibition to cause intentional harm', '*détournement de pouvoir* (misuse of authority)', 'manifest disproportion of interests', and 'arbitrary action, unreasonable conduct and fraud'.

The author illustrates the first of these by the *Bering Sea* arbitration in 1982 and the oral arguments in that case of Sir Charles Russell. This case, which featured prominently in Bin Cheng's work, has already been discussed in Chapter 2[37] as demonstrating how malice extinguishes entitlements without the need to pronounce the words 'abuse of right'.

Détournement de pouvoir is a form of *lex specialis* and a paradigmatic instance of the truism that rights cannot be exercised beyond the inherently vested authority. One does not need the 'rule' of abuse of right in order to hold, as the arbitral tribunal did in the *Lalanne Ledour* case of 1902 – cited by Kolb[38] – that the President of Guyana was abusing his rights when he prevented the import of cattle by one of his private commercial competitors.

If disproportionality is an outcome-determining principle of international law, it should perhaps be proposed as a self-standing rule rather than evidence of a rule prohibiting the abuse of rights. The cases cited by Kolb involve the collision of rights – perhaps better referred to as the presence of competing claims – which *do not really involve any abuse at all*, but simply the objective problem of what international law must seek to do when faced with the impossibility of overlapping rights to be exercised in mutually exclusive ways. It is telling that Kolb's invocation of 'a robust vision' is nothing less than the audacious thesis put forward by Hersh Lauterpacht in 1933 and discussed at some length in Chapter 6. The answer must be found in the interpretation of the pertinent texts, or (better yet) the promulgation of *lex specialis*.

Finally, Kolb himself acknowledging that arbitrariness, unreasonable conduct, and fraud 'to a large extent have become autonomous from the concept of abuse of rights'.[39] And it does not help to quote the use of these words in instruments like the Covenant of Civil and Political Rights; they are, once again, *lex specialis* and do not require us to accept Kolb's invitation to excursions into what he calls 'the polymorph galaxy centered on good faith and the prohibition of abusive action'.[40]

---

[36] Kolb, *Good Faith in International Law*, p. 142.
[37] See the third part of Chapter 2.
[38] Kolb, *Good Faith in International Law*, p. 143.
[39] Kolb, *Good Faith in International Law*, p. 145.
[40] Kolb, *Good Faith in International Law*, p. 145.

The Danger of Stray Phrases

The 'polymorph galaxy' derives its unmanageable contours from the observation often made in these pages to the effect that the word 'abuse' is ceaselessly used with different meanings and for different purposes that should be properly limited by their context. The phrases in which it appears are thereafter enlisted to serve in quite different ways. In the absence of the distinctions of careful analysis, this hampers the sober and difficult task of developing reliable general principles of law to serve as rules of decision in international fora.

A multitude of commentators fall into this trap – especially those who deal succinctly with the rubric of 'abuse of right' as a small part of a broader inquiry. Such is the case with Kolb, as it is with Charles Kotuby and Luke Sobota, the equally respectable co-authors of *General Principles of Law and International Due Process*,[41] a valuable monograph that nonetheless provides a couple of useful examples of the danger of reading too much into isolated phrases.

After quoting Planiol's dismissive *bon mot* regarding the 'logomachy' of abuse of rights, Kotuby and Sobota perfectly express a core element of the thesis of this book when they write this:

> It is true that, in most cases, an abuse of rights could be recast in terms of the party acting without any right at all. For example, under international law, a State has no power to expropriate except where necessary and in the public interest; nor can a State, consistent with the national treatment standard, exercise its regulatory powers so as to protect domestic producers from foreign competition.[42]

In fact, the authors implicitly make the case for concluding that the notion is unnecessary, yet nevertheless defend its status as a general principle. It should be noted that their monograph seeks to canvass all general principles, quickly dealing with abuse of rights in a section only slightly exceeding four pages. In so doing, they seem to have relied on pronouncements with respect to its status by other commentators, who not infrequently commit the fundamental error of perceiving something momentous every time they see the ordinary word 'abuse' in an award or a judgment. More often than not, a closer reading of the decision does not support the conclusion that it sets out anything that can be called a principle, except in the most nebulous sense.

---

[41] C. Kotuby and L. Sobota, *General Principles of Law and International Due Process* (Oxford University Press, 2017).

[42] Kotuby and Sobota, *General Principles of Law and International Due Process*, p. 113.

It is instructive to take two examples Kotuby and Sobota give as endorsements of significant claims. This requires going into the matters in some detail, and to keep this book to a manageable length, this cannot be done in every instance. The lesson to be derived is that the discussion of abuse of rights all too often does not take the discussion into any depth at all, and that this should be kept in mind by the discerning reader.

The first example is their statement that 'the principle' of abuse of right is 'frequently cited by the ICJ'. Their sole reference is to the *Fisheries Case* of 1951, involving the UK's unsuccessful challenge to coastal baselines claimed by Norway.[43]

Here, as in so many instances, this contention requires inferring a 'principle' of abuse of rights from an isolated use of the word *abuse* – in this instance, by way of criticising a *hypothetical* abusive contention with respect to the characteristics of a coastline. The Court observed that the rule on coastal baselines 'is devoid of mathematical precision . . . one cannot confine oneself to examining one sector of the coast alone, except in case of manifest abuse'. The Court immediately went on to say that *it was not faced with any abuse*; it upheld Norway's defence of its claimed baselines, accepting that 'the divergence between the baseline and the land formations is not such that it is a distortion of the general direction of the Norwegian coast', and concluded that Norway's construction of the line was 'moderate and reasonable'. One need only say that the obiter dictum is anything but a dispositive holding to the effect that an unsuccessful contention about a map could amount to the abuse of a right.

The second example is the (sole) reference they give in support of the contention that the principle has also been 'applied' by arbitrators in investor-state disputes – namely, *Saipem* v. *Bangladesh*.[44] There, an Italian contractor had brought an ICC arbitration in Dhaka, heard by three internationally well-known arbitrators, in pursuit of contractual claims against the state-owned entity Petrobangla. Displeased by a number of procedural decisions by the arbitral tribunal, Petrobangla obtained the judicial revocation in Dhaka of the arbitrators' authority. The arbitrators nonetheless proceeded with the case and rendered an award in favour of Saipem, ordering payment by Petrobangla of some

---

[43] *Fisheries Case (United Kingdom v. Norway)*, judgment, 18 December 1951, *I.C.J. Reports* (1951), 116, 141–2.

[44] *Saipem S.p.A.* v. *People's Republic of Bangladesh*, ICSID Case No. ARB/05/07, award, 30 June 2009.

USD 7 million. That award was declared a nullity by the Bangladeshi courts.

Saipem thereafter brought an ICSID arbitration against the State of Bangladesh under the bilateral investment treaty between Bangladesh and Italy on the grounds that its right to payment, as 'incorporated' in the ICC award, had been expropriated by unlawful decisions of the Bangladeshi courts.

Having found that Saipem's right to payment under the ICC award were 'expropriable rights' and that the court ruling to the effect that the award was a 'nullity' amounted to an expropriation under the Treaty, the ICSID Tribunal examined the bona fides of the decisions of the Bangladeshi courts. Saipem argued that 'grossly unfair, arbitrary, unjust or idiosyncratic' court rulings constituted a violation of international law. The ICSID arbitrators observed that the ICC arbitrators' authority had been revoked because of their supposed 'misconduct', and then held that for its part it 'did not find the slightest trace of error or wrongdoing' and that the revocation of authority could 'only be viewed as a grossly unfair ruling'.[45] They added: 'The judge simply took as granted what Petrobangla falsely presented.'[46]

Given these findings, the reader might expect that this was about to emerge as a textbook case for denial of justice.[47] A claim of denial of justice could not have been defeated on the grounds of failure to exhaust local remedies, since the arbitrators were of the clear view that further recourse would be an 'improbable' remedy.[48] Yet denial of justice was not one of the grounds for the decision, perhaps due to restrictions of the treaty on the scope of actionable claims.

Instead, the arbitrators gave two legal bases for their Award. One of them was perfectly straightforward: a violation of Article II of the New York Convention on the Recognition and Enforcement of Foreign Arbitral Awards in the form of an improper exercise of the supervisory authority of the courts of the place of arbitration.

---

[45] *Saipem S.p.A.* v. *People's Republic of Bangladesh*, ICSID Case No. ARB/05/07, award, 30 June 2009, para. 155.

[46] *Saipem S.p.A.* v. *People's Republic of Bangladesh*, ICSID Case No. ARB/05/07, award, 30 June 2009, para. 157.

[47] The quoted passages in the previous paragraph justify precisely that outcome; see J. Paulsson, *Denial of Justice in International Law* (Cambridge University Press, 2005), pp. 205–6.

[48] International law does not require the exhaustion of futile remedies. Paulsson, *The Denial of Justice in International Law*, pp. 115–19.

> It is the Tribunal's opinion that a decision to revoke the arbitrators'
> authority can amount to a violation of Article II of the New York
> Convention whenever it *de facto* 'prevents or immobilizes the arbitration
> that seeks to implement that [arbitration] agreement' thus completely
> frustrating if not the wording at least the spirit of the Convention. *This is
> indeed what happened here.*[49]

This is a direct invocation of a dispositive rule of international law. Yet,
strangely enough, this was not the first ground put forward by the
Tribunal, which (as though intent on innovation) instead gave precedence to this one:

> It is generally acknowledged in international law that a State exercising
> a right for a purpose that is different from that for which that right was
> created commits an abuse of rights.
> ... the Tribunal is of the opinion that the Bangladeshi courts exercised
> their supervisory jurisdiction for an end which was different from that for
> which it was instituted and thus violated the internationally accepted
> principle of prohibition of abuse of rights.[50]

Only one authority is cited for the confidently asserted foundational
proposition in the footnote to first of these two sentences – namely,
Alexandre Kiss. The footnote commences with the word 'for example',
ostensibly backing up the claim of what is 'generally acknowledged'. Yet, as
we have seen in some detail in the second part of this chapter, those
familiar with his doctoral thesis and locus classicus, *L'abus de droit en
droit international*, know that Kiss is ultimately not an authority for abuse
of rights as a general principle. The citation given is not to Kiss's book,
which as shown above is very circumspect in its approach to the possible
diffusion of the notion of abuse of rights *as an objective of legislation*.
Instead, the arbitrators make a rather unsatisfactory reference to Kiss's
brief entry on the topic (without quoting any words from it) in 'Berhadt
(Ed.) [sic], *Encyclopedia of Public International Law* Vol 1 at 5'.[51]

Having embraced the notion of abuse of rights as a principle, Kotuby
and Sobota gamely seek to justify it notwithstanding their own above-

---

[49] *Saipem S.p.A.* v. *People's Republic of Bangladesh*, ICSID Case No. ARB/05/07, award,
30 June 2009, para. 167. Emphasis added.

[50] *Saipem S.p.A.* v. *People's Republic of Bangladesh*, ICSID Case No. ARB/05/07, award,
30 June 2009, para. 160–1 (footnotes omitted).

[51] This is evidently intended to direct the reader to the work edited by Rudolf Bernhardt,
whose editorship ceased in 2001, and which has since appeared in various subsequent
editions as the *Max Planck Encyclopedia of Public International Law* published by Oxford
University Press.

quoted demonstration of its redundancy.[52] They give two rationales.[53] First, 'the exercise of a legal entitlement must ... be measured on its own terms and relative to other pertinent legal interests, which is exactly what the abuse of rights doctrine [*sic*] does'. This is sensible, indeed probably a truism, but does not produce a rule of decision; it identifies an indispensable consideration in the process of law-making – *the collision or conflict of rights*, which long ago was suggested by Desserteaux (see Chapter 1) as the true core of our subject: a call to action by the law-maker, not to ever-expanding judicial discretion.

The second is quite a stretch: 'The phrase "abuse of rights" ... goes some way in capturing the perniciousness of the wrong. ... It is precisely the beguiling invocation of a legal entitlement that makes the conduct so abusive and corrosive.' One doubts that the law bestirs itself to assign to losing parties any additional opprobrium for making 'beguiling' contentions. The mere assertion of unfounded entitlements (which one might say takes place in every single case where there is a losing party) is hardly sufficient to corrode the rule of law; the contention is simply rejected.

---

[52] See note 42.
[53] Kotuby and Sobota, *General Principles of Law and International Due Process*, p. 113.

The notion of abuse of right as an autonomous principle of international law continues to exercise a facile appeal. Yet international economic arbitrations have failed to yield a lex mercatoria capable of providing comprehensive rules of decision; this is not where a coherent principle of abuse of rights will emerge. A different proposal is to establish abuse of rights as a general principle derived from international law itself (rather than by the distillation of general principles common to national laws). This too founders on the observation that acontextual abstractions do not yield meaningful criteria amenable to predictable application, and that in any event international disputes may be, and have been, resolved in other ways. The modern international environment is abrim with concurrent rights that must be accommodated by negotiation or by properly enacted lex specialis without resorting to the provocative declaration of any of them to be abusive in its exercise.

8

The Vanishing Prospect

Noble Equity, we might say, has an evil twin. His name is Arbitrariness, and he goes everywhere in disguise, passing himself off as Equity. No one speaks with greater fervour of the virtues of fairness – and of the glory of unfettered discretion in the resolution of disputes.

In some fortunate communities, Equity is loved more than Arbitrariness is feared. The people know all of the latter's masks and recognise him by the smallest discrepancies of tone and expression; they read his motives like an open book and avoid him. They have no trouble identifying the real Equity.

The heterogeneous international community is more fearful – more distrustful, perhaps, of its own ability to tell the twins apart. This fear presents a challenge to the development of international law, and perhaps most of all to the legitimacy of its most meaningful manifestations – the institutions intended to transform principles into effective remedies and thus to contribute crucially to a culture of compliance.

Some proponents of international law, impatient with its lacunae and the difficulties of treaty negotiation, invite us to entrust judges and arbitrators with the broadest powers. They are in effect eager to bring Equity onto the stage. They likely prefer that no one worry too much whether the right twin actually appears in a given case. *Believe in Equity*, they seem to implore us; *in the long run, he will dominate, ensuring just outcomes in the interest of the world community.* This approach has not met great success, but not, as we shall now see, for want of exploring various avenues.

A Principle Generated by International Economic Arbitration?

International commercial arbitrations and treaty-based investment arbitrations involve parties and arbitrators of different nationalities. The international character of such disputes is precisely what makes it seem natural to identify rules that are appropriate for cross-border transactions, thus avoiding the need to apply a national law that may impose unexpected and inapposite technicalities. International transactions may moreover have specificities unencountered in the purely national space. Some parties may resist laws that are foreign to them as a matter of principle. States, in particular, tend to resist being judged by the laws of another nation.[1]

Two much-discussed ways to avoid the domination of national laws are (1) empowering arbitrators to decide on the basis of equitable considerations rather than as a matter of law, and (2) stipulating the applicability of an international *lex mercatoria*. It is instructive to consider how modest the contribution of these techniques has been in practice and why this is so.

For many generations now, it has been understood that in principle states and other parties who agree to international arbitration may specify that the tribunal is authorised to decide the dispute without being bound by rules of law. The arbitrators would thus act, in the commonly used French expression, as *amiables compositeurs*, or in accordance with what is 'right and good' (*ex aequo et bono*). They are empowered to make decisions based on what they believe to be fair, or perhaps merely *useful in the circumstances* in the sense of permitting a practical *modus vivendi*, without concern for the constraints of law. Their verdict is nonetheless endowed with the same degree of finality as that accorded to any other arbitral award.

Yet this option is in reality chosen by very few international disputants. Although Article 38(2) of the Statute of the International Court of Justice affirms 'the power of the Court to decide a case *ex aequo et bono* if the parties agree thereto', the Court has never decided a case exclusively

---

[1] Every treaty-based investment arbitration involves at least one state party. In the context of contractual disputes, 143 states or state entities were claimants or respondents in the 842 cases commenced in 2018 before the International Court of Arbitration of the International Chamber of Commerce, the leading international arbitral institution for commercial matters (involving 2,282 parties from 135 countries); see 'ICC Dispute Resolution 2018 Statistics' (ICC Publications, 2019).

based on this provision – very likely, as one writer has put it, 'being concerned that *ex aequo et bono* decisions might have all too strong political implications and thus diminish the authority of the ICJ in its strictly law-based judicial function'.[2] As for international commercial arbitration, a well-known treatise suggests that such clauses are found in not more than 2 or 3 per cent of contracts.[3]

Deciding on the basis of equitable considerations is not the same thing, since equity may be an explicit feature of law in various defined ways. When the relevant law expressly allows the final outcome to be affected by the adjudicators' sense of the fairest result in the circumstances, the decision is by definition within the law. The best-known example in public international law is the equitable adjustment of equidistant lines in maritime delimitation. Any law or treaty may grant such discretionary powers to adjudicators. In exercising that discretion, the adjudicators may well explain their decision as they see fit – for example, that they perceive themselves as preventing abuse. That does not per se create a precedent for the existence of a legal principle of 'the prevention of abuse of right'.

For its part, *lex mercatoria* is conceived as a possibly self-sufficient body of legal rules applicable to decide disputes arising out of international transactions. (Reliance on usages that may be specifically relevant to international transactions is something far more modest; national commercial law often looks to custom and usages, and there is no reason why the usages of cross-border trade should be excluded – without altering the fact that a national law is being applied.) Its best-known proponents, who came to the fore half a century ago, were Clive Schmitthoff and Berthold Goldman.[4] The variety of the suggested sources of *lex mercatoria* is open-ended: trade usages and customs, general principles of law; uniform model laws and international conventions regulating international commerce; public international law; comparative studies of national laws, rules, and judgments; standard contracts issued by internationally active entities; and published arbitral awards.

Although the debate was exhilarating and thought-provoking, it cannot be said that it won the day, or that many parties were prepared to stipulate to the applicability of *lex mercatoria* to their contracts – let alone that many arbitrators applied it on their own initiative. To understand why, it is sufficient to read one of the best-known essays on international

---

[2] M. Kotzur, 'Ex Aequo et Bono', in R. Wolfrum (ed.), *Max Planck Encyclopedia of Public International Law* (Oxford University Press, 2009).

[3] G. B. Born, *International Commercial Arbitration*, 2nd ed. (Wolters Kluwer, 2014), p. 2770.

[4] See generally T. E. Carbonneau (ed.), *Lex Mercatoria and Arbitration*, rev. ed. (Transnational Juris Publications, 1998).

commercial arbitration in the second half of the twentieth century, namely Michael Mustill's *The New Lex Mercatoria*.[5] Lord Mustill, a prominent English barrister, international arbitrator, judge, co-author of the standard English treatise *Mustill and Boyd Commercial Arbitration*, and leader of the English delegation at UNCITRAL during the elaboration of the Model Law on International Commercial Arbitration, may have had no equal as an arbitration specialist on the highest court of England and Wales. Although his stated aim was to 'examine [the mercatorist] position rather than to attack it',[6] he expressed these fundamental doubts:

> How could the arbitrators or the advocates who appear before them amass the necessary materials on the laws of, say Brazil, China, the Soviet Union, Australia, Nigeria, and Iraq? How could any tribunal, however cosmopolitan and polyglot, hope to understand the nuances of multifarious legal systems? In published awards the arbitrators occasionally make large claims about the universality of principles, but these are rarely if ever substantiated by citation of sources. Equally if no more important is the question: how could any adviser hope to predict what a tribunal not yet constituted might make of such a task in the future?[7]

After the word 'systems' in this passage, Mustill inserted this footnote:

> In the literature, the use of legal encyclopedias is sometimes advocated. I suggest that these are usually worse than useless for this particular purpose, unless the reader is guided by someone with direct knowledge: a little learning is indeed a dangerous thing. Anyone with practical experience of international disputes must acknowledge the difficulty of making an accurate assessment of the law of only one unfamiliar legal system, absent the kind of prolonged and expensive legal guidance which would be quite out of the question if dozens of different laws had to be assimilated.

Attempting to identify 'the rules of *lex mercatoria*', Mustill came up with twenty of them. This list had the comical result of causing the enthusiasts of *lex mercatoria* to praise him to the skies; for years, countless speakers at international conferences would invoke his name to say that '*even* Lord Mustill', a common lawyer of great renown, had admitted that *lex mercatoria* contains no less than twenty important rules. This was an outrageous mischaracterisation – but sometimes repetition takes on

[5] M. J. Mustill, 'The New *Lex Mercatoria*: The First Twenty-five Years', in M. Bos and I. Brownlie (eds.), *Liber Amicorum for Lord Wilberforce* (Oxford: Clarendon Press, 1987), p. 149.
[6] Mustill, 'The New *Lex Mercatoria*', n. 5.
[7] Mustill, 'The New *Lex Mercatoria*', p. 156.

an undeserved authority, and so Mustill was enrolled against his own words as an adherent to the cause.

In fact Mustill's list was explicitly prefaced by introducing it as 'rules which are *said to* constitute the *lex mercatoria* in its present form'.[8] Anyone reading them can only conclude that those who referred to the list as an endorsement of the concept had not actually read the essay. For example, item four reads: 'There may be a doctrine of *culpa in contrahendo*' and ends with a footnote that asserts flatly: 'The doctrine is not known to the common law.' Item ten appeared with this comment: 'Perhaps in some cases either a gold clause or a "hardship" clause may be implied', and this time the footnote records that a frequently quoted arbitral 'precedent' had asserted that the common law is *'plus accessible à la revision de contrats en cas de déséquilibre'* (more tolerant of the revision of unbalanced contracts), which Mustill archly dismissed as 'not a correct statement of the common law'. Similarly, he waved off item twenty ('Failure by one party to respond to a letter written to it by the other is regarded as evidence of assent to its terms') as 'not consistent with the common law'.

Among the few 'rules' that he cited without particular objection, one finds item five: 'A contract should be performed in good faith'. But this maxim is doubtless just what he had in mind when citing Professor Schlosser to the effect that 'whilst there can be an abundance of sweeping formulations of legal principles, these are of little use for legal analysis'.

All in all, this amounted to 'rather a modest haul';[9] Mustill concluded by questioning 'whether the foundations of the *lex mercatoria* are sound enough to sustain the blasts to which it may be subjected'.[10]

He added that he did 'not wish to end on such a negative vein', but then continued to express views that were hardly complimentary for *lex mercatoria*. The 'growth and strengthening' of international arbitration, he opined, does not depend on its success. In commercial disputes, the outcome 'in most instances' is determined by what the contract provides and what the facts are found to be. If law is required, it is 'nominated in the contract'.

Mustill was, it seems, quite right. Although the theory and the desirability of *lex mercatoria* as applicable law in international transactions may be debated endlessly, the practical reality is that it is very seldom adopted in contractual governing law clauses. This should give pause to those who favour the resolution of disputes by arbitrators unfettered by rules of law. It

[8] Mustill, 'The New *Lex Mercatoria*', p. 174.
[9] Mustill, 'The New *Lex Mercatoria*', p. 177.
[10] Mustill, 'The New *Lex Mercatoria*', p. 182.

seems that those who exercise their freedom to go to arbitration nevertheless want the discipline and predictability they perceive in the enforcement of defined rights and obligations. The romance of *lex mercatoria* has faded.

For present purposes, one notes that while Mustill mentioned 'the general principles of law' as one of seven sources of *lex mercatoria*, 'abuse of right' was not part of the list of twenty 'rules'. Yet it would fit right in, since they too are expressed at a high level of expression, and have also echoed in varied and unstable specific applications here and there, in one jurisdiction or another.

This is not the end of the story of *lex mercatoria*, and certainly not a denial of the usefulness of thinking about it. After all, it might be said that the 1980 United Nations (Vienna) Convention on Contracts for the International Sale of Goods is the relatively successful realisation of a project to recreate a significant part of *lex mercatoria* as an embodiment of national law. The great effort that resulted in the yet more ambitious UNIDROIT Principles of International Contracts merits acknowledgement as well (although it should be noted that it too failed to endorse the concept of abuse of right[11]).

In this light, if the notion of abuse of right were allowed to develop unchecked into a justification for unfettered discretion, it may well resemble an arbitral power grab: the usurpation of authority to decide by fiat. Consider this sequence:

1. Arbitrators mandated to decide in accordance with a given law nevertheless *declare* that according to their research the law in question is composed of a number of general principles.

2. Next, they *declare*, still according to their research, that abuse of right is such a general principle.

3. Then they *find* that a claim or defence based on a particular right is not in accordance with 'the purposes for which that right was established' or 'violates the sense of proportionality', and therefore one party or the other, whatever may be their preference – loses under the *principle* of abuse of right.

4. Finally, since the arbitrators say that they are acting in accordance with their interpretation of the applicable law as containing the principle of abuse of right – even only 'in spirit' or 'by implication' – the decision is presented as being within their authority and therefore unappealable.

---

[11] See the more extensive discussion on the various editions of the *Commentary on the UNIDROIT Principles of International Commercial Contracts (PICC)* in the third part of Chapter 1.

Is this a desirable outcome to be pursued? If so, will it work, against the howls of indignation from losing parties, and the reaction of controlling jurisdictions to whom they will address their complaint? The virtue of rules of precedent may be described as that of an 'anti-arbitrariness vaccine' inasmuch as decisions are justified by an ex ante standard, but if the notion of precedent is taken to the extreme of legitimising any outcome arbitrators deem fair and just, it may well do the opposite, and develop into an epidemic of arbitrariness. Parties will be disaffected, and flee when they can.

A Principle Generated by International Law Itself?

Chapter 5 introduced an alternative to the discouraging project of distilling a general principle from national laws to serve as a feature of international law – namely, the promotion of a general principle of abuse of right generated exclusively in the sphere of international relations. The example described there was Helmut Philipp Aust's proposal to rely on just such a category of general principles as the foundation of the rules of complicity in the law of state responsibility. It is instructive to consider his reasoning, but first – and even more interesting – it is useful to examine the broader canvas of G. D. S. Taylor's effort to identify specific applications of an autonomous international principle. This attempt is *rara avis*, and therefore merits careful consideration.

Taylor published an article in 1973 under the title 'The Content of the Rule against Abuse of Rights in International Law'.[12] The title reveals that the author assumes the existence of a *rule* – as opposed to a theory, notion, truism, platitude, or what have you. Indeed, the first sentence of the article is this: 'That no person may abuse his rights has long been accepted in theory as a principle of international law.' This assertion (citing chapter 14 of Lauterpacht's *The Function of Law in the International Community*, but nothing else) immediately elicits the objection that this abstract notion is less than useful as a rule of decision. That is precisely the point that Taylor sought to address when announcing an examination of *the content of the rule*.

He proposed for the purposes of his study that the word 'right' should be replaced with 'discretion', and that accordingly the presence of legally unacceptable 'abuse' could properly be examined in accordance with

---

[12] G. D. S. Taylor, 'The Content of the Rule against Abuse of Rights in International Law', 46 *British Yearbook of International Law* (1972–3), 323.

general principles of administrative law. The exercise of discretion may be challenged only 'if the law recognizes certain principles upon which that discretion must be exercised'.[13] Discretion may also *expressis verbis* be created as absolute. But if the discretion in question expressly or impliedly identifies the matters that decision-makers should bear in mind, they abuse it unless they (1) pay heed to those matters and (2) disregard irrelevant ones.

The aptness of the analogy with administrative law is perhaps subject to argument, as may be the equiparation of 'right' with 'discretion'. But it seems useful to suspend criticism at the theoretical level and see how this conceptual framework might function in practice. If it yields attractive results, it may have promise and deserve development. So we turn to the applications proposed by the author.

The study began with unreviewable conduct. This includes, in Taylor's phrase, 'plenary governmental power',[14] the decision whether to espouse the international claims of a national,[15] and 'self-judging reservations to the International Court's compulsory jurisdiction'.[16]

Next, Taylor presented three illustrations of the ways in which an abuse of right might be inferred. First was *Electricity Company of Sofia and Bulgaria* (Preliminary Objection),[17] involving a claim of abuse in the timing of the denunciation of a treaty (to avoid litigating a dispute that was already ripe). This point was dealt with in the dissenting opinion of Judge Anzilotti, who rejected the claim with a brain-teasing treble negative: the circumstances were not such that no reasonable state would have renounced the treaty at that moment if it was not motivated by evading the obligation.

---

[13] Quoting the formulation in *Associated Provincial Picture Houses Ltd.* v. *Wednesbury Corporation*, [1948] 1 K.B. 223, at 228.

[14] The example Taylor gives is this: the Permanent Court of Justice did not purport to question whether the Ottoman Parliament complied with its own Constitutional requirement that a piece of legislation be 'expedient' in *Lighthouses Case (France* v. *Greece)*, judgment, 17 March 1934, *P.C.I.J.* Ser. A/B, No. 62.

[15] 'There are no matters which are irrelevant to the State's decision how to deal with a national's claim. There are no reasons which would be legally improper. There can be no review for abuse of right.' See Taylor, 'The Content of the Rules against Abuse of Rights in International Law', 328.

[16] 'Neither bad faith nor any other ground of abuse of right is available to overrule a State's invocation of its self-judging reservation.' See Taylor, 'The Content of the Rules against Abuse of Rights in International Law', 331.

[17] *Electricity Company of Sofia and Bulgaria (United States* v. *Cuba)*, preliminary objection, judgment, 4 April 1939, *P.C.I.J.* Ser. A/B, No. 77.

Then came *Walter Fletcher Smith,*[18] where a sole arbitrator held that the Cuban government had abused its right to expropriate when 150 men had come onto Smith's property and torn down the buildings the day after a 'preliminary' court order, and the land was handed over by municipal authorities to a favoured local person to use for his own profit.

Third was *Chuinard* v. *European Organization for Nuclear Research,*[19] where an unsatisfactory staff member whom the Organization wanted to demote failed to persuade the ILO Administrative Tribunal that the suppression of his post was an abuse of right. Although it was impermissible to use the power to suppress posts as a way of dismissing an employee, the Tribunal rejected the claim because the staff member had been offered an alternative though lower position that it considered that a reasonable employee would have accepted.

These examples are hardly convincing as proof of the implicit acknowledgment of a notion of abuse of right, for all three cases could have been (and indeed were) resolved without it. It is sufficient to state a positive rule to the effect that once a state has acceded to a treaty it may not denounce it when faced with an actual ripe dispute. Similarly, there is no right to expropriate otherwise than in the public interest. And it seems that Chuinard's demotion was justified by criticisms of his performance, and therefore could not be deemed a constructive dismissal.

Taylor suggested the following conduct as suitable for testing against the criteria of abuse of right: (1) errors of municipal law so gross as to indicate bad faith and thus denial of justice, (2) acts that would defeat the object and purpose of an unratified treaty under Article 18 of the Vienna Convention on the Law of Treaties, and (3) the manipulation of movement of inhabitants in advance of a plebiscite.[20] Yet each of these issues involve assessments of the performance of obligations in good faith that can be examined and disposed of without recourse to a notion of abuse of right, indeed without mentioning the word 'rights'. (Moreover, the international law with respect to denial of justice already deals with instances of gross errors of municipal law.[21]) And while Article 18 of the Vienna Convention, like most national civil codes, requires good

---

[18] *Walter Fletcher Smith Claim (United States* v. *Cuba),* award, 2 May 1929, 2 *R.I.A.A.,* 913.

[19] *Chuinard* v. *European Organization for Nuclear Research,* Judgment No. 139, decision, 3 November 1969, 53 *I.L.O. Official Bulletin* (1970), 153.

[20] *The Tacna-Arica Question (Chile* v. *Peru),* award, 4 March 1925, 2 *R.I.A.A.,* 921.

[21] J. Paulsson, *Denial of Justice in International Law* (Cambridge University Press, 2005), pp. 82–3.

faith in the performance of obligations, this standard is applied contextually in its broad terms, without the support of subsidiary principles.

The case of *Right of Passage over Indian Territory* (Merits)[22] is a useful illustration of the potential collision of concurrent sovereign rights. Portugal had the right to convey civilians over Indian territory to its colonial enclaves on the subcontinent, and India had the right to regulate that traffic. This was precisely the type of situation, in the view of supporters of the theory of abuse of right, that establishes its usefulness. But it seems that the phrase *abuse of right* was never uttered, and the matter was resolved by examining the objective justification for the challenged intensity of regulation to determine whether it was pretextual. (Most similar situations arising under international law are likely to arise under a treaty containing sufficiently detailed terms to be applied in accordance with its terms, construed if necessary by resort to the Vienna Convention.)

Right of Passage is discussed in a section of Taylor's article devoted to improper purposes. It addresses a number of other contexts in which the need for an autonomous principle of abuse of right is no more persuasively established than in *Right of Passage*. For example, improper purposes in the context of claims of wrongful expropriation or discrimination are in modern international law examined against the backdrop of extensive specific jurisprudence that (to take the case of expropriation) does not need to invoke abuse of right since it is sufficient to find that an expropriation is not justified by 'public utility'. To examine the matter by reference to the notion of abuse would, given its irreducible indeterminateness, create needless confusion. Taylor contended that administrative law has been 'unable to prescribe any general limitation of object' by which to measure the 'public interest'.[23] Whether or not that is true in particular national systems, the fact is that international tribunals must, and do, apply this test.[24] Moreover, abandoning the criterion

---

[22] *Right of Passage over Indian Territory (Portugal v. India), merits, judgment, 12 April 1960, I.C.J. Reports* (1960), 6.

[23] Taylor, 'The Content of the Rules against Abuse of Rights in International Law', 339–40.

[24] To take a single example among a multitude, see Article 4(2), Germany-Afghanistan BIT: 'Investments by investors of either Contracting State shall not directly or indirectly be expropriated ... except for the public benefit ...'. Some treaties include clarifying footnotes indicating that public purpose refers to a concept of international law or customary international law; see e.g., Article 10.10, n. 10–9, Peru-Singapore FTA. For just two among many instances of application, see *ADC Affiliate Limited and ADC & ADMC Management Limited* v. *The Republic of Hungary*, ICSID Case No. ARB/03/16,

of 'public utility' in favour of 'abuse of right' hardly produces greater clarity.

Taylor similarly suggested that claims of wrongful discrimination on the grounds of nationality could also be viewed through the prism of abuse of right. But discrimination is a well-traversed subject in international law, and examined under equally well-known criteria: 'objective and reasonable' justification for the distinctions made, along with a reasonable degree of proportionality between means and ends.

Taylor's article concluded by illustrating his proposition (to the effect that abuse of right should be viewed as abuse of discretion) by imagining how such a new conception of abuse of rights might have been applied in the actual, then-recent *South West Africa* cases in which the Republic of South Africa's mandate in what is now Namibia was challenged on the basis that the RSA had misused governmental competence.[25] The example seems ill-chosen. As the author himself put it, 'The way the case was

award, 2 October 2006, paras. 429–33. The tribunal found no public-interest justification for the takeover of the airport terminals by the state, stating, in particular:

> 430. Although the Respondent repeatedly attempted to persuade the Tribunal that the Amending Act, the Decree and the actions taken in reliance thereon were necessary and important for the harmonization of the Hungarian Government's transport strategy, laws and regulations with the EU law, it failed to substantiate such a claim with convincing facts or legal reasoning.

> 431. The reference to the wording *'the strategic interest of the State'* as used in the Amendment Motion by Dr. Kosztolányi does not assist the Respondent's position either. While the Tribunal has always been curious about what interest actually stood behind these words, the Respondent never furnished it with a substantive answer.

> 432. In the Tribunal's opinion, a treaty requirement for 'public interest' requires some genuine interest of the public. If mere reference to *'public interest'* can magically put such interest into existence and therefore satisfy this requirement, then this requirement would be rendered meaningless since the Tribunal can imagine no situation where this requirement would not have been met.

See also *Marvin Roy Feldman Karpa* v. *United Mexican States*, ICSID Case No. ARB(AF)/99/1, award, 16 December 2002, paras. 135–6. The dispute concerned application of tax laws to export of tobacco products; the tribunal – albeit finding that there was no expropriation and expressing reluctance about giving excessive weight to the public purpose criteria – determined that there were rational public purposes, notably to discourage cigarette smuggling, as well as to prevent inaccurate or excessive claims for rebates, for the Mexican policy of requiring invoices to provide tax refunds.

[25] *South West Africa (Ethiopia* v. *South Africa; Liberia* v. *South Africa)*, preliminary objections, judgment, 21 December 1962, *I.C.J. Reports* (1962), 319; *South West Africa*, second phase, judgment, 18 July 1966, *I.C.J. Reports* (1966), 6.

argued and the way in which the Judges dealt with the submissions on the merits indicate that neither counsel nor the Judges really understood the roles they were required to play.'[26] In fact, the Court made no determination of abuse of discretion, one way or the other. Moreover, the 'power' in question was not an inherent right of states, but one conferred by a UN trusteeship mandate; this means that it concerned a type of legal principle that actually 'has no general field of operation in State action'.[27]

Still, perhaps *faute de mieux*, using this sole example and proposing 'the correct analysis' [*sic*], Taylor referred to the RSA's obligation under the mandate to promote the well-being and progress of the inhabitants and asserted that it put the spotlight on improper reasons for actions by the RSA (the priority given to 'European' education and the prevalence of various forms of discrimination were 'directed toward the factual annexation of the territory') and 'would arguably constitute an abuse of right'.[28]

Taylor concluded by noting that this 'view of abuse of rights' is 'certainly not' what Lauterpacht had described, but rather a systematization and extrapolation of the common concept of abuse of right.[29] This 'systematization' by employing an analogy with administrative law and abuse of discretion will not persuade everyone (indeed perhaps very few), but is interesting to assess as a path to rules of decision for concrete cases. What it reveals is that without exception the many controversies chosen as examples may be resolved without recourse to the over-arching abstraction 'abuse of rights'. We may well be left with the impression that for some reason the study followed an a priori impulse to find a place for the doctrine even if it is not necessary, and even at the cost of displacing available rules of decision – something like an indulgent aunt intent on inventing a job in her business for a favourite but unproductive nephew.

Moreover, Taylor noted that the type of abuse of right that 'reaches the furthest and possesses the greatest scope for growth' – namely, 'use of power for a reason that was not one for which the power was conferred ... has no general field of operation in State action. For it to operate there must be a conferred power set out with some measure of precision. Few State powers are conferred'.[30]

---

[26] Taylor, 'The Content of the Rules against Abuse of Rights in International Law', 345–6.
[27] Taylor, 'The Content of the Rules against Abuse of Rights in International Law', 342.
[28] Taylor, 'The Content of the Rules against Abuse of Rights in International Law', 348–50.
[29] Taylor, 'The Content of the Rules against Abuse of Rights in International Law', 350.
[30] Taylor, 'The Content of the Rules against Abuse of Rights in International Law', 341–2.

Four decades later (and explicitly referring to Taylor), Aust considered the utility of the concept of abuse of right when applied to the particular topic of state responsibility for complicity in international delicts. In doing so, he takes us back to Lauterpacht, one of whose central *Leitmotifs* was the need for 'material completeness' of the international legal order; the absence of rules of decision is intolerable, and they must somehow be generated to fill the void. The progressive – if not instant – development of the law, Lauterpacht believed, could and should be accelerated by reference to the concept of abuse of right, as explained in a remarkable passage that put his proposal in a nutshell:

> It is consonant with State sovereignty to refuse to recognize any source of liability other than that grounded in consent given by treaty or in a rule of law evidenced as binding by custom. But that limitation of liability to defined categories may not be consistent with justice and with the requirements of law in a progressive society. Conduct which has hitherto been in accordance with the purpose of law may cease to be so owing to developments which the law has not yet time to take into account: behaviour which the law is as a rule content to regard as not in contradiction with social needs ceases to be so when the advantage accruing to one party from the exercise of an otherwise legal right results in disproportionately grave injury to others; action which is described as lawful may cease to be so if pursued in an unsocial manner or in a manner contrary to the purpose for which it has been allowed. *In all these cases such conduct, while* prima facie *lawful, amounts to an abuse of a right conferred by the law.*[31]

How might this apply to a quintessential modern problem of public international law – namely, that of *concurrent, competing* rights? Consider again the degree to which a state may claim exclusive rights to determine what is or is not permitted in its territorial sea. We leave aside situations in which the solution is set out in a treaty. (Even in a treaty, there may be a claim of exception, be it a matter of national security or another form of necessity.) The answer then, to follow Lauterpacht, is centred on the question whether a prohibition imposed by the coastal state is an abuse of sovereign rights, and that in turn depends on whether it causes 'disproportionately grave injury' or is 'pursued in an unsocial manner or in a manner contrary to the purpose for which it has been allowed'. The discretion of the adjudicator to weigh the facts in light of these subjective criteria reigns supreme.

---

[31] H. Lauterpacht, 'General Rules of the Law of Peace', in E. Lauterpacht (ed.), *International Law: Being the Collected Papers of Hersch Lauterpacht*, vol. I, *The General Works* (Cambridge University Press, 1970), p. 384. Emphasis added.

Aust's subject was state responsibility for complicity in wrongful acts by another state, not the consequences of excessive claims of competing rights. As a building block to the construction of a framework to deal with complicity, Aust begins as follows: 'One possible technique to solve these conflicts of colliding rights is the application of abuse of rights.'[32] This is an attractively modest phrasing, and Aust immediately notes[33] 'the skeptical position in this regard' staked out by Roulet.[34] The approach is *possible* – but is it good, and is there something better?

First one wonders why Aust did not simply point to Article 16 of the International Law Commission's Articles on State Responsibility ('ASR'), which provides that a state may be 'internationally responsible' for aiding or assisting another state in the commission of an internationally wrongful act, and say that ASR 16 reflects international law. After all, the ILC is formally charged with the codification and progressive development of international law.

The reason seems to be the author's discomfort at the thought that the Articles are explicitly intended to constitute 'secondary' rules, which unlike primary, 'substantive' rules, do not establish obligations under international law but rather consider the consequences of the established breach of primary rules. This is a problem, in Aust's view, because 'there is general agreement that, before the adoption of the ASR, international law did not provide for a general rule against complicity. . . . Without the rule embodied in Article 16, one might conclude that States would be largely free to help other States violate international law.'[35]

This is a curious preoccupation, given that Aust already observed, three pages previously, that the ICJ in 2007 recognised that ASR 16 'reflects customary international law'.[36] Apparently this recognition was not sufficient because, as Aust writes, 'the exact contours of this rule remain unclear'.[37] If that is the rub, how do we deal with it? It seems this is where the 'principle' of abuse of right comes in, not in the narrow sense that Taylor derives from equating 'rights' with 'discretion', but in

---

[32] H. P. Aust, *Complicity and the Law of State Responsibility* (Cambridge University Press, 2011), p. 69.

[33] Aust, *Complicity and the Law of State Responsibility*, n. 97.

[34] See the extended quotation in Chapter 2, note 11.

[35] Aust, *Complicity and the Law of State Responsibility*, p. 6.

[36] Aust, *Complicity and the Law of State Responsibility*, p. 3, referring to the *Case Concerning Application of the Convention on the Prevention and Punishment of the Crime of Genocide (Bosnia and Herzegovina* v. *Serbia and Montenegro)*, judgment, 26 February 2007, *I.C.J. Reports* (2007), 43, para. 419.

[37] Aust, *Complicity and the Law of State Responsibility*, p. 3

the full-blown Lauterpachtian (if not indeed the extreme Josserandist) vision.[38]

Concretely, one would thus begin with the enquiry whether a particular instance of state conduct offends Lauterpacht's abstract criteria (disproportional injury, 'unsocial manner', conflict with the purpose of a right), and ultimately hold that sovereign actions that aid or assist the commission of an internationally unlawful act is an abuse of the prerogatives of sovereignty.

To be blunt, surely this fits the familiar expression of scratching your left ear with your right hand. We already know that ASR 16 forbids complicity (with the understanding that there must be a predicate ascertainment of the wrong-doing with which the respondent is said to be complicit). If we need more granularity – for example, whether it is necessary that the assisting state is conscious of the objectives pursued by the main actor – this will have to await clarification developed in jurisprudence. Such is the inevitable and proper consequence once a principle is established in international law. The particular contexts in which such a principle is examined will yield apter rules of decision than anything that would emerge from assigning the entire exercise to a far more general notion ('abuse of rights') in its irreducible abstraction.

Aust introduces his work by announcing: 'We will find that there is sufficient practice to speak of a general rule against complicity in the law of State responsibility. We will also be able to establish the necessary *opinio juris*.'[39] He goes on to do just that, in a well-documented and persuasive manner. But the twenty-seven pages[40] devoted to bringing abuse of right into the picture are an unnecessary and unhelpful distraction. Indeed, the exercise concludes with a disclaimer: 'We need not and cannot take a position on these suggestions. Rather, we will turn to an assessment of international practice and see whether positive international law provides an answer in this regard.'[41]

In the end, after a careful and insightful account of state practice, Aust concludes that the collision-of-rights situation cannot be solved 'by recourse to the principle of abuse of rights which is ... vague and

---

[38] The former considered that there was an abuse of rights every time 'the general interest of the community is injuriously affected' by insistence on a 'less important ... individual right'; see Chapter 6, note 6; the latter contended that the 'legitimacy' of the notion of abuse of rights was essential to 'the destiny of law'; see Chapter 2, note 20.

[39] Aust, *Complicity and the Law of State Responsibility*, p. 7.

[40] Aust, *Complicity and the Law of State Responsibility*, pp. 69–96.

[41] Aust, *Complicity and the Law of State Responsibility*, p. 96.

would not present a significant step forward in the direction of a legal system which offers differentiated responses to such situations'.[42] It is accordingly important that his very useful monograph not be construed as an attempt to revive the ambitious idealism of Politis and Lauterpacht.

True, the vast literature of international law contains incidental references to abuse of right as a limitation of such prerogatives as the authority to alter rates of exchange or other measures affecting the value of money, the liberty to carry out upstream riparian activity, and the freedom of use of the high seas (e.g., in laying cables). The problem is that the expression 'abuse of right' as a limitation is far too nebulous, and in effect seems to give arbitrators the power to decide in accordance with their personal policy preferences. These matters are more soundly dealt with by the processes of negotiation and accretion of custom backed by *opinio juris* – no matter how frustrating the former may be, and how gradual the latter.

Imagine judges who simply say that 'we refer to the general principle against wrongful behaviour' and on that sole basis reject a party's position. In such a situation, one would obviously not expect criticism by an appellate jurisdiction to the effect that 'there is no general principle that parties should not engage in wrongful behaviour', but rather a holding that the invocation of such an amorphous standard does not provide the legal basis required for the dismissal of a legal contention. In other words, the recognition of a *ratio decidendi* must depend on a minimum of intellectual discipline to establish criteria that prevent an abstract expression from becoming an excuse for arbitrariness, and allow any case to be decided any way.

The International Court of Justice gave an example of its characteristically great prudence with respect to newly claimed 'general principles' in *Obligation to Negotiate Access to the Pacific Ocean (Bolivia v. Chile)*, the judgment in which it rejected an attempt to invoke *legitimate expectations* as a foundation of state responsibility.[43] Just as there is universal rejection of the abstract notion of abuse of rights, so we are all prepared to uphold legitimate expectations. (Indeed, the very words assume the conclusion; 'abuse' is bad, 'legitimate' is good.) Yet they are simply too indeterminate to constitute rules of decision. Giving legal effect to the

---

[42] Aust, *Complicity and the Law of State Responsibility*, p. 423.
[43] Obligation to Negotiate Access to the Pacific Ocean (Bolivia v. *Chile)*, preliminary objections, judgment, 24 September 2015, *I.C.J. Reports* (2015), 592; *Obligation to Negotiate Access to the Pacific Ocean*, merits, judgment, 1 October 2018.

terms of a validly concluded treaty is of course a way of vindicating legitimate expectations, but *pacta sunt servanda* is already a rule of decision and the reference to expectations is as unnecessary as an addition as it is insufficient alone.

The circumstances were the following. Bolivia has been landlocked for well over a century, and has long sought access to the sea. Bolivia argued that Chile had so often manifested its readiness to accommodate Bolivia's desire that the latter was entitled to rely on legitimate expectations of obligatory negotiations that would lead to sovereign access. But the problem was a never closed gap; Bolivia wished to expand its unqualified sovereignty to the coast, whereas Chile at various times expressed its preparedness to envisage the conditional grant of practical accommodations such as free transit, a duty-free port, and the like; or else strips of territory that were less than Bolivia demanded, or subject to conditions like quid pro quo ceding of Bolivian territory, or demilitarization. Bolivia nevertheless insisted that the 'principle' of legitimate expectations has been 'widely applied in investment arbitrations'.[44] In its initial memorial, it had maintained that

> [a] State is entitled to consider that it is concluding a binding international commitment if the nature of the text, viewed objectively, is such that a party in good faith would understand that text as embodying an international legal commitment. In those circumstances, applying the principle of good faith and legitimate expectations, the party that made the declaration cannot plead its lack of intention to make a legal commitment.[45]

Chile countered by insisting that 'no rule of international law . . . holds a State legally responsible because the expectations of another State are not met'.[46] The Court upheld Chile's position. It did not identify any of the 'investment arbitrations' invoked by Bolivia, let alone set out the criteria (if any) endorsed by the arbitrators in question. Its entire rationale for dismissing Bolivia's argument in this respect is set out in the following single paragraph:

> 162. The Court notes that references to legitimate expectations may be found in arbitral awards concerning disputes between a foreign investor

---

[44] Obligation to Negotiate Access to the Pacific Ocean, merits, judgment, 1 October 2018, para. 160.

[45] Obligation to Negotiate Access to the Pacific Ocean, memorial of the government of the Plurinational State of Bolivia, 17 April 2014, para. 334.

[46] Obligation to Negotiate Access to the Pacific Ocean, rejoinder of the Republic of Chile, 15 September 2017, para. 2.33.

and the host State that apply treaty clauses providing for fair and equitable treatment. It does not follow from such references that there exists in general international law a principle that would give rise to an obligation on the basis of what could be considered a legitimate expectation. Bolivia's argument based on legitimate expectations thus cannot be sustained.[47]

To seek to justify an outcome by invoking the notion of abuse of right would likely be even more problematic. The present boundary between Bolivia and Chile was established by the 1904 Treaty concluded in the wake of the War of the Pacific. Bolivia did not, however, attempt to pursue an argument to the effect that Chile's failure to accede to Bolivia's desire for access was an abuse of right established by that Treaty. It is indeed hard to see how insistence on rights of general sovereignty can be wrongful; such claims are either well founded or not. As for harm caused by the exercise of sovereignty, such as the pollution of waters that flow into a neighbouring country, it is another matter, but – once again – best resolved not by invoking abuse, but rather positive obligations created by international agreements, or interpretation of the inherent limits of rights in specific contexts.

On the other hand, given the impossibility of agreeing with Shakespeare's Shylock (because rights do not survive their abuse),[48] we can surely live with the notion of abuse of rights as an *objective* of law-making, perhaps usefully extended by considerations suggested long ago by Cheng himself as the conclusion of his discussion of abuse of rights.[49]

[47] As to whether foreign investments are protected by a principle of legitimate expectations applicable under treaties, see the contrasting views of E. Snodgrass, 'Protecting Investors' Legitimate Expectations', 21 *ICSID Review: Foreign Investment Law Journal* (2006), 1, and M. Paparinskis, *The International Minimum Standard of Fair and Equitable Treatment* (Oxford, 2013), pp. 252–9. Some cases (although a very small percentage) under the Convention on the Settlement of Investment Disputes between States and Nationals of Other States arise out of contracts between states and investors, and they may contain clauses stipulating the applicability of a national law. If so, there may be a debate (probably difficult enough in and of itself) as to the existence, and if so as to the criteria, of a principle of abuse of right under that national law. But arbitrations under international bilateral or multilateral investment agreements are by definition creatures of treaty, and thus by nature expressions of *international* law.

[48] The general right to rely on a contract would succumb to finding that Shylock's specific contractual remedy (the pound of flesh) was unenforceable. The common law notion of 'unconscionable terms' seems more satisfactory than that of an 'abuse of right'. We can all agree that irrespective of our legal cultures Shakespeare's example is not worth much attention as a matter of the law of contract, since the merchant would – in any civilized county – have been arrested for assault the moment he acted to secure his stipulated 'remedy'.

[49] 'All rights have to be exercised reasonably and in a manner compatible with both the contractual obligations of the party exercising them and the general rules and principles of the legal order. They must not be exercised fictitiously so as to evade such obligations or

But such generalities cannot substitute for *lex specialis*. As we shall now see, it would be an unnecessary mistake for European law to employ abuse of right as a rule of decision.

'Abuse of *Law*?'

The last part of Chapter 1 mentions the lengthy collection of essays entitled *Prohibition of Abuse of Law? A New General Principle of EU Law*[50] published in 2011, consisting of the contributions of twenty-six writers addressing an ostensibly common theme of 'abuse of law'. In considering the problem of their abuse, it is unhelpful to equate the concepts of rights and law. (The former deals with unrighteous claims of entitlement in general; the latter is focused on attempts to subvert particular legislation.) As noted, twenty-one of the chapter titles in the book refer to 'abuse of law', and only five refer to 'abuse of rights'.

The legal issues treated under the heterogeneous banner of these essays include the free movement of goods and services, broadcasting, employment, company law, insolvency, the common agricultural policy, international civil procedure, and those dealt with in no less than eleven contributions concerning 'abuse of law' in the particular area of taxation. It seems quite obvious that most of the authors considered the body of laws of the particular domain that they were addressing, and then expressed a view as to what claims under those laws would be considered abusive – without any concern for the conceptual justification for treating the exercise as part of a vast undertaking to derive a unified concept of abuse of law, let alone any attention to the reductionist objection (inevitable in the mind of an attentive reader) that the *lex specialis* which the authors invite us to apply (if administered in the way they propose) already does the same work as the prohibition of abuse of right, and (assuming competent deliberations and drafting) in a far more predictable way.

So, what most of these contributions, in fact, do is to set out the issues and solutions as to how the *lex specialis* suitable for the particular context of laws and regulations would define and counteract abuse. This is all fine and good. What is less productive is something that most of these authors

---

rules of law, or maliciously so as to injure others.' See B. Cheng, *General Principles of Law as Applied by International Courts and Tribunals* (Cambridge University Press, 1953; paperback, 2006), p. 136.

[50] R. de la Feria and S. Vogenauer (eds.), *Prohibition of Abuse of Law: A New General Principle of EU Law* (Hart Publishing, 2011).

did not do (and some indeed warned against),[51] namely to seek to project all such efforts into a single theory purporting to lead to abstract rules available to adjudicators even in areas where there is no law that defines indispensable rules of decision, thus leading to undisciplined ad hoc rule-making of the sort that mature legal systems (and the best judges) abhor.

Yet the volume ends with a concluding fifty-page essay by Vogenauer entitled 'The Prohibition of Abuse of Law: An Emerging General Principle of EU Law', of which the final two paragraphs announce 'an emerging general principle' to the effect that 'a given rule of law will not be applied' when these two criteria are met: the result would be 'contrary to the purpose of that rule', and the reliance placed on it is abusive.[52]

The European Community has articulated its rejection of abuse of right – for example, in Article 17 of the European Convention on Human Rights and Article 54 of the Charter of Fundamental Rights of the European Union. The latter provides: 'Nothing in the Charter shall be interpreted as implying any right to engage in any activity or to perform any act aimed at the destruction of any of the rights and freedoms recognized in this Charter or at their limitation to a greater extent than

---

[51] See e.g. J. Gordley, 'The Abuse of Rights in the Civil Law Tradition', in R. de la Feria and S. Vogenauer (eds.), *Prohibition of Abuse of Law: A New General Principle of EU Law* (Hart Publishing, 2011), p. 33: 'Antonio Gambaro has called "abuse of rights" a "doctrine without a future" in private law. One should hope this is right, given the doctrine's past and present. The French jurists … formulated it … in order to build a critique of nineteenth-century formalism. The doctrine found supporters in France and later in Germany, not because of the merits of this critique, but despite its flaws. It promised to be a vehicle for political and social change. The doctrine survived, not because this promise was fulfilled, but because it was forgotten. In the case in which it has been applied, the doctrine is not grounded on any distinct notion of "abuse". "Abuse" is a label applied to conduct when there is some independent reason for thinking the conduct is objectionable. Even if this were not so, and even if one could identify a concept of "abuse" that explains when conduct is immoral or impinges unjustifiably on others, one wonders how much light it could shed on the right was to reconcile national systems of taxation and regulation with EU principles of free movement of goods, capital and persons.' (Gambaro is quoted in Chapter 1, note 5.) Having adopted this stance, quite in line with that adopted in this book, Gordley then makes something of a *volte-face*: 'Should we conclude, then, that the European Union should not adopt a doctrine of abuse of rights? Certainly not. We can only conclude that the European Union should not borrow such a doctrine from private law. Because the problem that the European Union faces are quite different from those of private law, it may well be that some new and different doctrine of abuse of rights may be useful in resolving them. But it will have to be new and different.' Perhaps it is enough for a reader to have reviewed the brief Chapter 3 to conclude that this is unlikely to happen, and the attempt would produce only confusion.

[52] Feria and Vogenauer, *Prohibition of Abuse of Law: A New General Principle of EU Law*, p. 571.

is provided herein.' Who could argue that laws may be interpreted so as to allow the 'destruction' of fundamental 'rights and freedoms'?

As for the European Court of Justice, it has notably referred to 'the general Community law principle that abuse of rights is prohibited', and immediately explaining:

> Individuals must not improperly or fraudulently take advantage of provisions of Community law. The application of Community legislation cannot be extended to cover abusive practices, that is to say, transactions carried out not in the context of normal commercial operations, but solely for the purpose of wrongfully obtaining advantages provided for by Community law.[53]

Again, who would disagree? Yet there is less here than meets the eye, as should be clear if one considers the words 'improperly', 'fraudulently', and '[sole] purpose of wrongfully obtaining advantages'. Where is the principle or rule that allows a citizen, or a lawyer being consulted about the apparent 'advantages' of a Community law, or a judge asked to rule on actual conduct, to decide whether these essential characterisations apply?

The question is whether such general pronouncements are addressed to decision-makers in individual cases, or as an admonition to legislators that they should take care to draw lines that reflect the proper 'limitation' of rights and freedoms. The latter is suggested by Article 54 itself by the words 'provided herein'. There is no invitation to a judicial free-for-all, and indeed one of the contributors to the collection makes clear that since its appearance in 2000, Article 54 has had little impact.[54]

Indeed, Vogenauer's lengthy concluding essay, which begins by quoting the just-reproduced passage from *Kofoed*, immediately admits that 'the preceding chapters will have shown that the precise scope, contents, and limits of the prohibition of "abuse of law" or "abuse of rights" are far from being settled'.[55]

Moreover, those who take the trouble to read *Kofoed* will find that it confirms the limited use (and possible danger) of decontextualized quotations of handy maxims found here and there in judicial

---

[53] Case C-321/05, *Hans Markus Kofoed v. Skatteministeriet* [2007] ECR I-5795, para. 38.

[54] A. Arnull, 'What Is a Principle of EU Law?', in R. de la Feria and S. Vogenauer (eds.), *Prohibition of Abuse of Law: A New General Principle of EU Law* (Hart Publishing, 2011), p. 22.

[55] Feria and Vogenauer, *Prohibition of Abuse of Law: A New General Principle of EU Law*, p. 521.

pronouncements. Indeed, the judgment supports the principal thesis of this book, as we shall now see.

To constitute a proper precedent of the possibility of a claim of abuse of rights as a general principle without more specific legislative warrant, the rationale of the case must be a finding of an abuse of right on that elevated ground. What the reader will find is that *Kofoed* was a 'reference for preliminary ruling' concerning an issue of the taxation of corporate mergers and acquisitions. Interpreting a European Council Directive on the 'common system of taxation' intended to avoid distortion within the EC, and in particular to treat corporate restructuring as a non-taxable event, the European Court of Justice, in fact, *rejected* the Danish Tax Ministry's position.

In a nutshell, Mr Kofoed and an associate were each 50 per cent shareholders in a Danish company that became a subsidiary of an Irish company when the two men exchanged their shares in the Danish company for shares of the Irish company (also 50 per cent each). Shortly thereafter, the Irish company paid a substantial dividend to its shareholders that exceeded 10 per cent of the value of the (Danish) shares given up by Mr Kofoed. The relevant Directive (90/434) allows an untaxed cash payment that is ancillary to such an exchange of shares, but only within that 10 per cent limit. Mr Kofoed resisted the Danish tax authorities' insistence that the fact that the dividend exceeded that limit meant that the exchange of shares was not tax-free. The question put to the Court was whether the Directive was to be interpreted

> as meaning that there is no 'exchange of shares' within the meaning of the Directive where the persons involved in the exchange of shares, at the same time as agreeing to exchange the shares in a non-legally binding manner, declare it to be their common intention to vote, at the first general meeting of the acquiring company after the exchange, in favour of distributing a profit in excess of 10% of the nominal value of the security transferred by way of the exchange of shares and such a profit is in fact distributed?

The Court concluded that there was no evidence that the dividend in question 'formed an integral part of the necessary consideration' to be paid by the Irish entity and therefore in principle did not reverse the tax-free characterisation of the exchange. But then it went on, at the behest of the Danish government, to consider whether there might be an abuse of right in that the transaction was structured in a manner that 'was not carried out for any commercial reason whatsoever but solely for the purpose of achieving tax savings'. Whether this could create an exception to the non-taxable characterisation of the exchange of share would be a matter for the relevant (Danish) national law, provided that it was 'sufficiently precise and clear and that the persons concerned are put in a position to know the full extent of their rights and obligations', a Danish court would then be in a position to determine whether the case was one of tax evasion or avoidance and therefore an abuse of the European Directive.[56]

Where does this leave us? Vogenauer observes:

> From 1990 onwards, the legislative organs of the Union began to enact provisions of specific kinds of abuse in particular areas of EU law, such as the taxation of exchanges of shares between companies from different Member States, the use of EU budget resources, the cross-border transmission of broadcasting services, international civil procedure, the right to reside in another Member State, the measures to ensure the enforcement of intellectual property rights and value added tax.[57]

His view, however, is that these 'instances of secondary legislation are sporadic and narrow ... "codifications" or "reflections" of the broader prohibition that [the Court] has developed in its case law'.[58] Indeed, this apparently unintentional description of an unadulterated acceptance of the primacy of judge-made common law (which would only be proffered with substantial reservations by a modern English lawyer) may be precisely backward in the European context, where judges will look *first* at the *lex specialis* that tells them how to decide, and not to consider such laws secondary, always to be corrected by other judges who know how to understand and decide what to do with the elevated, abstract norms that articulate the fundamental aims and limits of legislation.

---

[56] *Kofoed* is not a solitary case, nor is tax the only field in which the notion of abuse of rights has been invoked by European judges. For instance, in Case C-110/99, *Emsland-Stärke GmbH* v. *Hauptzollamt Hamburg-Jonas* [2000] ECR I-1595, I-1615, the European Court of Justice decided that the shuttling of materials from Germany into Switzerland and back again for the purpose of recouping an export refund was abusive because it was contrary to the purpose of the refund rule and carried out with the intent or seizing unfair advantage. Why did this have to be called an abuse of right? The law-makers had apparently not thought it necessary to specify that the shuttling of goods back and forth across borders did not qualify as 'exports' and should not generate gains, and one can only wonder why the judges could not simply have confirmed that overwhelming conclusion of common sense.

[57] Feria and Vogenauer, *Prohibition of Abuse of Law: A New General Principle of EU Law*, pp. 522–3.

[58] Feria and Vogenauer, *Prohibition of Abuse of Law: A New General Principle of EU Law*, p. 523.

One can only imagine the confusion that would have been created if, instead of issuing detailed Directives on Unfair Terms in Consumer Contracts, the European Community[59] had simply proclaimed (perhaps on a constitutional level) that it is an abuse of rights for consumer contracts to be enforced if their terms are 'unfair', and then leave the matter to judges.

Vogelauer's final sentences are perhaps at once anticlimactic and reassuringly modest (and one wonders how three words encapsulating an abstraction could ever become more than 'embryonic' until they are assimilated into positive legislation):

> [T]his general principle is still emerging. It awaits universal recognition. Some of its doctrinal foundations are still shaky. The conceptual framework is not yet consistent. As might be expected from an 'embryonic principle', its emergence raises normative concerns: the prohibition has the potential of endangering legal certainty, the proper division of powers between the judiciary and the legislature, the rule of law, the uniform application of and effectiveness of EU law and the overriding goal of market integration. The Court has met these concerns by subjecting the prohibition to carefully crafted limits: it 'continues to use the notion of abuse with considerable restraint – and rightly so'.[60]

Concluding Observations

We may leave as an open question whether the quality of justice overall is better served by an abstract generality that can then be invoked to justify the good sense of a wise judge on an ad hoc basis, or as the starting point for the painstaking development of distinctions in a body of precedents. However, in the particular case of *abuse of right*, the former is too nebulous to provide rules of decision, and the latter is too marked by the specificities of the common law, which moreover not infrequently develops in significantly varying strands in different jurisdictions.

Still, however elusive they might be, the words 'abuse of right' are very much a part of civil lawyers' vocabulary and therefore should mean something. Is there a core sense so useful, or so compelling, that it should be deemed a general principle even though it is foreign to the common law?

---

[59] Starting with Council Directive 93/13/EEC of 5 April 1993.
[60] Quoting AG Poiares Maduro in Case C-210–06, *Cartesio Oktato es Szolgaltato bt* [2008] ECR I-9641, para. 29.

Law should be predictable. If we know that a given conduct leads to a foreordained consequence, we can act serenely in accordance with that understanding and not have to fear arbitrary outcomes.

Yet we often achieve only approximations. The finest legal minds cannot give precise definitions that would allow us to know at once when conduct has, for example, crossed the border to *negligence*, or gone even further and deserves to be treated more severely as *wilful* negligence. The universe of circumstances to be evaluated is both infinite and expanding. At some extreme point, it seems that in most legal systems judges may resort to something like an inherent authority to 'avoid injustice', even when faced with an explicit rule that would otherwise lead to a result they find intolerable in the light – as they see it – of some higher, overriding imperative.

These unremarkable observations set the stage for the suggestion that although such corrective notions are unavoidable, they should be treated with caution. They tend to be simple, but nebulous and abstract. *Fairness, good faith, proportionality* – no one questions them as values. It takes no legal learning to be fervently attached to them, to feel confident when invoking them, to throw them onto the table like trump cards. But in the hurly-burly of life, such compelling abstractions tend to be nothing more than the beginning of argument – their application to troublesome facts is controversial, the outcome unpredictable. We cannot allow adjudicators to decide cases according to personal policy preferences ostensibly justified by the simple invocation of an amorphous value judgment – uncontroversial and indeed platitudinous in its generality, but by itself inapt as a rule of decision.

The fact that a multitude of legal texts frequently use the word 'abuse' when affirming sentiments like 'it is important to ensure that rights are not abused' is not evidence of a general principle of abuse of rights. In fact it rather demonstrates a very broad objective that requires law-makers and regulators to carefully set out contextually meaningful limitations on rights which are susceptible to abuse. When that is done properly, Planiol's *bon mot* is all that needs to be said; the problem has been solved because 'the right ends where the abuse begins'.[61]

---

[61] In the 1907 edition of his treatise, Planiol wrote the following: 'For if the use of a right is to be condemned as antisocial, it must be the case that it has no other goal but to cause harm to another; as long as the acting party may perceive a personal advantage, its conduct is licit, for otherwise the use of any right would be impossible; commerce, competition, social progress, the development of human energy comes at this price. But this means that the judge must examine parties' conscience, to determine and weigh their motivation; the

Adjudicators, meanwhile, should be loath to base their decisions on abstractions dressed up as 'principles' with the pretence that they are rules of decision. As Justice Oliver Wendell Holmes memorably affirmed on the bench of the US Supreme Court: 'General principles do not decide concrete cases.'[62] Privately, he could be more provocative. In a letter to his friend Harold Laski, Holmes wrote that in deliberations he would tell his fellow Justices that 'no case can be settled by general propositions. . . . I will admit any general proposition you like and decide the case either way'.[63]

The problem is that such notions may be universally agreed yet fail to indicate how to decide because of a lack of specificity that the adjudicator cannot provide without, in effect, *acting as law-maker for a single case* and thus running the risk of being accused of arbitrariness if not partisanship. It has been the aim of this book to show that *abuse of right* is precisely such a dangerous concept.

This conclusion already arises in the *static* perspective of the few immediately preceding paragraphs. It is strengthened when one views it in a *dynamic* perspective, because the unquestionable need to curtail the abuse of rights by *lex specialis* is amplified over time, on pace with the increasing complexity and interrelatedness of modern communities.

This is a consideration of relevance not only to international law. The law of the Netherlands is known for its focus on achieving equity, and might therefore have been expected to give a significant role to an autonomous doctrine of abuse of rights. Yet more than four decades ago the Dutch scholar Chris Brunner reached a different conclusion in his survey of decided cases, and in so doing made a cogent observation. The accretion of granular legislation in response to the complexities of modern society, it seemed to him, was in reality leaving *less* room for the notion of abuse of rights:

> There is a natural tension between the freedom of the individual to pursue his own interests when exercising his rights, and the interests of others who are harmed thereby. Also, the general interest makes its own demands. The balance struck between these conflicting interests differs from country to country and from time to time. To protect the general

psychological aspect becomes dominant. One must fear that civil law thus takes on a task beyond its means.' See M. Planiol, *Traité élémentaire de droit civil* (Librarie générale de droit et de jurisprudence, 1907), p. 285.
[62] *Lochner* v. *New York*, 198 U.S. 45, 76 (1905) (Holmes, J., dissenting).
[63] Letter of 19 February 1920, in R. Posner (ed.), *The Essential Holmes* (University of Chicago Press, 1992), 38.

interest, specific legislation has abounded in the Netherlands over the last 50 years, so that the individual's free exercise of his rights has been substantially restricted. In a densely populated country, such as Holland, legislation limiting the permitted use of real property understandably takes first priority. Within the limits set by such legislation, the predominant view, as reflected in the tests applied by our courts for abuse of rights, remains that the individual may largely pursue his own interests as he sees them. The interests of others play only a minor role: they may not be completely disregarded by the person who exercises his right, but his right comes first by a wide margin.

This implies that the practical significance of the doctrine is rather limited.[64]

This passage rings all the more true in the ever-denser international environment, characterised by concurrent, overlapping, and in and of themselves perfectly legitimate claims of rights that need to be reconciled on a solid, predictable basis – and certainly not on the sole grounds of more or less intuitive assertions of abuse. This requires *lex specialis*, defining the limits of rights with specificity and therefore making it impossible to abuse them: they cease to exist, Planiol would be content to observe, outside their explicit limits.

[64] C. J. H. Brunner, 'Abuse of Rights in Dutch Law', 37 *Louisiana Law Review* (1977), 729 at 740.

INDEX

References such as '178–79' indicate a (not necessarily continuous) discussion of a topic across a range of pages. Wherever possible in the case of topics with many references, these have either been divided into sub-topics or only the most significant discussions of the topic are listed. Because the entire work is about 'abuse of right(s)', the use of this term (and certain others which occur constantly throughout the book) as an entry point has been minimised. Information will be found under the corresponding detailed topics. Page references in italics are to footnotes.

For EU product safety concerns, contact us at Calle de José Abascal, 56–1°,
28003 Madrid, Spain or eugpsr@cambridge.org.

www.ingramcontent.com/pod-product-compliance
Ingram Content Group UK Ltd.
Pitfield, Milton Keynes, MK11 3LW, UK
UKHW020351140625
459647UK00020B/2395